313

Life in the Motor City

John Carlisle

Charleston • London

THE
History
PRESS

313 | Life in

the Motor City

Published by The History Press
Charleston, SC 29403
www.historypress.net

All images are courtesy of the author.
Cover design by Karleigh Hambrick.

First published 2011

Manufactured in the United States

ISBN 978.1.60949.490.2

Library of Congress CIP data applied for.

Notice: The information in this book is true and complete to the best of our knowledge. It is offered without guarantee on the part of the author or The History Press. The author and The History Press disclaim all liability in connection with the use of this book.

Contents

Introduction

THERE'S NO PLACE like Detroit.

This city is wild and raw and unpredictable and eccentric. In Detroit you can grow a farm in your front yard, or keep goats and chickens out back, or throw a blues concert in the field next door, or buy a historic church for $100 and make it a museum. You can even operate a strip club in your living room. In an unexpected way, Detroit in its decline has become the land of opportunity. You can do all sorts of things here that you can't do elsewhere. But in many ways you're on your own.

Years of bad city government and corrupt elected officials have left the city broke. Now, residents can't get a timely response to most 911 calls, can't get the streetlights lit on their streets, can't get abandoned houses next door torn down. And in this void, a loose, do-it-yourself culture has evolved.

Some people decide that in the absence of the cops, they'll provide the neighborhood's protection. Some people mow the grass in the parks when the city won't cut it anymore, or plow the snow from their own streets when it's clear nobody else will. Some turn empty buildings into art canvases, while others will simply keep their own property looking nice, even when their neighbors don't, even though they wouldn't get in trouble if they didn't bother. Detroit is an unfinished experiment in what happens when most of what makes a normal city operate goes away.

The city's problems are now legendary. Almost two-thirds of the population has fled since it peaked in the 1950s. Most of the small businesses left too, followed by the big employers. High crime is a grinding reality. Half the city can't read. You could write a thick textbook about the social and personal irresponsibility of many of its people. The school system has collapsed, unemployment is rampant and city government has become ineffective at providing even basic services to its residents. And because of all this, thousands of those residents head for the suburbs every year.

Yet in so many ways the city is a triumph over all sorts of odds—of people over circumstances, of order over chaos, of persistence over resignation. The real Detroit isn't just some wasteland of poverty and drugs and crime and abandonment. It's also little bakeries and neighborhood watches and packed churches and outdoor fairs and history on every block. It's decent people somehow making it with what they have. Despite all the hardships the city is facing, Detroit still has residents doing little things to make their corner of the city work.

This is a book about some of those people.

The stories in *313* are about the people off the main roads and under the radar, the ones who never make headlines or draw much attention to themselves outside their neighborhoods. But they're the ones who keep the city going, with unglamorous acts and unnoticed gestures, behind the scenes, year after year.

There's a certain resilient hope among many Detroiters, a sense that you really can create your own world here, that things will get better because they can't get much worse. And from that idea comes a feeling of freedom to do what you wish with your life here. Because in Detroit, you can be just about anything you want.

The Hard Sell

An Entrepreneur Tries for Success on the Streets

DAYS LIKE THESE are long and tough.

Mr. Bow Tie stands by the curb along West Seven Mile at Greenfield, wearing bright red pants, a red vest and a crisp white shirt. And, of course, a bow tie.

You can't miss him because he shouts at passing traffic through a megaphone. Or he dances on the grass, whirling a sign in his hands, volunteering his skills. Sometimes he blurs by on his bicycle, pulling a wagon festooned with two banners advertising his work.

He's offering a single service—cleaning dirty headlights. Nothing else. Regardless of how the rest of the car looks.

"Once people understand I'm the go-to man for this service, I believe it's going to take off," says Malcolm Carey, the forty-three-year-old behind the Mr. Bow Tie persona. "I've got total faith in that."

Seven days a week, for hours at a time, he stands along the road and shouts the same polite, formal sales pitch at traffic:

"I am Mr. Bow Tie of Mr. Bow Tie's headlight restoration. I specialize in making those yellow, faded, ugly headlights look new again. If you know someone with yellow, faded, ugly headlights, tell them to come see me, Mr. Bow Tie, right here, right now. Thank you."

The cars whip by. A bus driver passing close to the curb gives him a thumbs-up. Someone honks, and a driver waves. But so far today, nobody's stopping to get their headlights restored.

The problem is most people don't think headlights need cleaning, or they don't have the time it takes or the twenty-five dollars it costs.

Mr. Bow Tie making his pitch along Seven Mile.

A car pulls into the Burger King parking lot behind him. A man and a woman get out. Carey springs over.

"What's up, my brother?" he says, animatedly. "I do headlight restoration. Can I clean your headlights?" The man agrees. Then Carey tells him it's a twenty-seven-minute process. He knows this because he always times himself. The yes becomes a no.

"We're not even gonna be here that long," the man tells Carey, walking away as he talks. "I thought you was going to be, like, fast, quick, in a hurry. We's about to order and go."

Some days go this way, Carey says. Long hours and few takers. "But then you have those days that makes up for it, when everything pops."

Mr. Bow Tie is among countless people in the city trying to make a living by offering some unique service or quirky talent to the public on the streets. It takes confidence and persistence and determination. And it's a hard way to earn money.

Carey heads back to the curb, summons his enthusiasm and begins talking into the megaphone again. "I am Mr. Bow Tie..."

HE WAS TWELVE when he fell in love with auto detailing, the thorough cleaning and polishing of a car inside and out. He was breaking bottles in an alley and a collision shop owner called him over and offered to pay him to instead sweep his shop's floors.

Soon after, the owner had just finished a paint job on a car and wasn't looking, and a curious Carey grabbed a buffer, went to work on the car and ruined the paint job. The owner went nuts. "But after he got finished cussing me out, he showed me how to do it correctly," he says. Detailing became his career. He still does it on the side.

The Mr. Bow Tie persona developed at the car wash where he last worked. He began dressing up to stand out on the line. "Everything there is about tips, so I'm trying to distinguish myself from all the other car washers in there who are walking around with baggy pants, dirt on all of them. But me, I got clean shoes, a clean outfit, I present a more neater appearance, so they prefer me working on the cars."

His headlight restoration business was born after trouble at work. Carey had so specialized his detailing craft that he eventually confined himself to working only on cars with black paint. The owner wasn't amused by this new policy.

"One day he had a red truck come in, and I refused to do it because he already knew I only do black, so we had a disagreement and he fired me on the spot," Carey says. "But that firing helped me out because then I had the opportunity to pursue my headlights."

A few minutes pass. A truck pulls up. "How's the headlights on your car, bro?" he asks a man who steps out from the driver's side. "They need to be freshened up?"

"You can," the man replies, "but I ain't got no extra bread right now." Another no.

Carey's face shows discouragement. "Of course, I'm not immune to that," he says about his spirits getting down. "When you figure out the secret to that, let me know."

IN HIS FIRST month on the job, Carey did all his cleanings for free, hoping word-of-mouth would lead to paying customers. Slowly, it did.

Some days he still resorts to it. "Normally what happens is, once I get one car, then they'll start coming over," he says. "I get that curiosity factor going. One customer has me on his car, and then they all start coming over."

This is one of those days. Carey starts approaching people in an Auto Zone parking lot, offering to clean headlights for free. The first one says no. Then another. But two men pull up in a beat-up pickup truck, and after hearing it's no charge, the driver agrees.

Finally, a yes.

It's an elaborate task. He sands both headlights four times with four different sandpaper grades, then applies a fuzzy buffing pad that's soaked in polish and attached to a cordless drill. Solvents are used to clean away the oils, then a cloth is used to shine it all up. Throughout the long job, he gives an eloquent presentation detailing each step.

He takes photos of his work, transfers them through a cable to a printer he's got hooked up to a battery and gives each customer a print showing the before-and-after difference of each headlight. After affixing his business sticker to the back, the job is done. Twenty-seven minutes.

"Hey, that's sweet," says the customer, eyebrows arched at the sight of the photo. "It's a big difference." It was free, but they give him five dollars anyway.

Suddenly, Carey's marketing theory proves right. As he's working, some people in the lot crane their necks; a few walk over to watch. Two young girls pull up in their red Grand Am, and they want the service. Things are officially picking up.

As he sands the first headlight, he looks at them and asks, with sincere curiosity, "What made you decide to give me a chance?" It's the tone of a man who's had a hard day.

"You looked like you knew what you were doing," one of them says. "We're just giving somebody a chance, somebody in the community that's doing something."

Mr. Bow Tie tends to a customer's dirty headlights.

It goes like that sometimes. People see a regular guy from their neighborhood earnestly trying to make it the honest way, working hard every day in the same spot, down on his knees, and a few will support him almost on principle, even if they don't have much money, even if they don't really need their headlights polished. There's just enough of them out here to carry his business until people agree with him that shiny headlights make any car look sharper.

"I just hope it survives," he says, "that I can keep doing what I'm doing. Sometimes the money don't flow, you know. Some days we eat good, other days we eat famine."

When he's done and the girls drive off, he's back to standing in the cold, without a jacket, waving his sign and shouting in his megaphone, hoping someone else sees him and gives him a chance.

And tomorrow he starts all over again.

A Day of Rest

The Back Room of a Little Detroit Shop
Becomes One Man's Oasis

THIRTY-THREE PRAYER BEADS lie strung in the loop that hangs softly in his hands. Thirty-three times he threads them between his finger and thumb, telling himself with each bead that God is great.

This is how Mogtaba Shirdel, known as Mike, passes the afternoon nowadays, in the quiet back room of his store, Mike's Antiques. It's a custom he brought with him from the old country.

"As you can see, nobody comes," says the seventy-year-old Iranian, pointing to his front door, which faces Morang Drive on Detroit's east side. "Maybe one or two, they just come in and walk and go."

Shirdel has the ways and looks of an Old World gentleman—dapper and traditional, yet gregarious and warm. He's got a thicket of salt-and-pepper curls, wears a loose wool scarf thrown gracefully around his neck and says things in a Persian accent with an elegant lilt.

Times are tight and business is slow. Gas bills are too high to put the heat on, so he wears a jacket and scarf when he's in the shop. Same goes for the electric bill, so he relies on the soft winter daylight that pours through the windows. And after twenty-three years here, his landlord has the building up for sale, making every day part of a countdown to a closing date that Shirdel doesn't yet know.

"It's just a hobby now, that's all," he says. He doesn't like being alone in his apartment all day, so he hangs around the shop, sipping Lebanese tea brewed in a charred teapot on an old stove in the corner. The voice of an Iranian television newscaster beamed here from halfway around the world shouts

Mike Shirdel with his prayer beads.

from the television. And he thumbs his beads, one by one, waiting for customers, waiting for the last day.

But he likes it like this. It took a lifetime before he could take it easy this way. You might not know it, seeing him sitting back with one leg softly draped over the other, but he spent most of his life working himself ragged, trying to make it in America, then just trying to make it.

LIFE IN TEHRAN was good until the mid-'60s, when his father's semi-truck business went bankrupt and the family went broke. Shirdel suddenly had to support two old parents and seven young siblings on a high school education. And there were few opportunities at home.

"You talk to the friends, they say America is a gold mine," he says. So he blindly came to New York City alone, at twenty-six, with $300 in his pocket and not a word of English in his vocabulary.

He slowly picked up the language by looking things up, one word at a time, in a thick Persian-English dictionary he took everywhere. He'd translate words he saw on subway posters or overheard on TV, or he'd pull it out when someone said something to him and painstakingly try to figure out what it meant. He still has it, all cracked spine and torn pages, on a shelf in the back room.

The man was born to work. His first job was at a textile plant, but then he took on extra jobs at coffee shops and restaurants and delis and a movie theater. He drove a cab, too, and later a limo. He'd even take one-day jobs through the local employment agency sometimes, just to earn a few more bucks.

"If you don't work hard, you don't get nowhere," he says. "You have to work, hard work. I done everything because I take care of my family, send them money," he says. "I always hustling."

At one time, three of his jobs overlapped, leaving him working from Friday at 6:00 a.m. to late Sunday night, with an hour break between each. He'd take naps in hotel lobbies or on the subway in the sliver of time between jobs.

This schedule soon unraveled. He once passed out head first onto the table at a restaurant during a date with a girlfriend, he says. Then he excused himself and took a nap in the bathroom. And there was the time he fell asleep for twenty-four hours straight without knowing it and missed a whole day of work. It cost him one of the jobs. He just went out and found another.

All the while, he'd pay his bills and send whatever money he had left back to his family in Iran. He didn't go to movies, rarely went out to eat, never went to clubs. He admits he missed out on a lot in life because of self-denial for his family.

"I do anything for them," he says, his eyes tearing up. "Anything. The family is the blood in you; it's something you cannot forget. You grow up together, you live together, you eat together, you sleep together. All of this stays with you, it's part of you. So if you can do something for them and you don't do it you're a disgrace to God. A lot of people don't understand that."

ONE DAY, A woman at the airport got into his cab. "I look at the mirror and she's looking at me in the mirror," he says with a wink. "I had the big curly hairs. I was young." They swapped phone numbers. Months later, he married her.

She was from Detroit and convinced him to move back here. Once again he plunged into work, starting a limo service and buying rental properties for income. He initially got the shop as storage space for things he'd need for his houses—screen doors, windows, toilets. After he'd cleaned it and carpeted it, though, he changed his mind. "I said, well, it's too good to put the toilets there." Instead, he started an antique shop with a few items he had on hand.

His marriage fell apart, and he lost his properties in the divorce, leaving him with little more than his store. He moved into it for thirteen years, living in the back room until just recently, settling into being an antiques dealer. But he sold it not long ago to pay some bills. In a few years, he went from being a landlord of several properties to a renter of one.

Now, after years here, he has the familiar Detroit misfortune of owning a shop in a neighborhood that started out one way and has now ended up another, very different way. Before, the area was middle class, and people living nearby had a taste for antiques or had old houses full of old things they'd sell him.

"Everywhere from all over the country they used to come, 'cause they know I have nice pieces. And then what happened is changes, change, change, so all the white [people], they scared and they moved out."

Pretty soon the neighborhood filled with new residents who didn't have much money or urge to buy his fine china, or antique oak dressers, or the coffee tables inlaid with marble.

Shirdel eventually amended his sign outside to say "Resale Shop" in a nod to the changes around him. He started selling some old clothes that people buy sometimes, but few customers browse the record albums, and books just don't get read by the residents living nearby. Meanwhile, the antiques go unsold unless a stray collector happens by the store, a place few outside the neighborhood know about, but a place where few from the neighborhood actually shop.

So a lifetime of hard work has finally wound down to a day like this one—a lone gentleman in a quiet room, immersed in the faint smell of antique wood and yellowed books, enjoying the pleasure of something as simple as sitting back for a while.

A woman rings the doorbell and Shirdel gets up, lets her in. She just moved a street over and came to browse for the first time. She doesn't buy anything, though.

"What is that accent?" she asks him.

"Persian," he replies.

"It's very exotic," she says. Her comment draws a charming smile from him.

After she leaves, the only voice heard in the cold room is that of the newscaster from back home. Shirdel goes back to his seat, sips his tea and draws his beads through his fingers. Thirty-three times once more.

Poletown Saints

A Beautiful 125-Year-Old Church Lives On
Despite Faith-Testing Circumstances

IT'S HARD TO hear the priest.

His voice has softened with age, he's got a thick Polish accent and his microphone keeps cutting in and out. Still, Father Edward Kaszak pushes forward with the Mass, a little in fluent Polish, some in halting English, giving the most unique liturgy in town.

There are only twelve parishioners seated in the pews at the front. There's room behind them for almost twenty-five hundred more.

It's Sunday at St. Albertus Catholic Church in Detroit's old Poletown. But this isn't an official church anymore; the Archdiocese of Detroit closed it twenty years ago. These infrequent Masses aren't sanctioned anymore; they're performed by the freelance priest who bikes in from Hamtramck, wearing black clothes and a backpack.

The lights are kept low during services to save money, so the church stays dim except when light pours through the stained-glass windows, bathing everything in soft colors. The heat is on just to keep the water pipes from freezing, so in winter the congregants inside wear winter coats.

The plaster in the 125-year-old church is chipping, the paint is peeling, scrappers have set upon the place with fervor and the only thing standing between it and destruction are the efforts of a handful of people who've devoted themselves to keeping a magnificent relic alive.

There's no place else like it in Detroit. The way its tattered beauty still shows despite its age, the way a handful of people keep it going despite the challenges, the way its past was wild and sometimes even violent—it's a lot like the city it has stood in all these years.

Brian Baka, guardian of the temple, sits by the mannequin of St. Stanislaus's corpse.

Life-size mannequins dressed in Easter garb stare out from all corners.

"This place is not only a statement about God; it's a statement about us," says Bob Duda, sixty-four, part of the Polish American Historic Site Association, the group that takes care of St. Albertus. "It's like a skyscraper—here we are folks, we're important, just as important as anybody else. We're going to be proud of ourselves. That's why they built churches like this; otherwise they could've done it in tents. It's a testimony to us and our history and our heritage."

St. Albertus has been here since 1872, when about three hundred immigrant families from Poland started the church in a small, wood-frame building with a single priest and his one-armed assistant, a veteran of the Polish Wars.

A new priest fresh from Poland, Father Dominic Kolasinski, came a few years later and rallied the parishioners to build a bigger church with a Gothic Prussian design, to remind them of the lavish, medieval churches they left behind in Europe.

Not long after the new church opened in 1885, the local bishop suddenly removed its charismatic priest and appointed a replacement. The congregation split into camps for and against the move. Kolasinski's supporters got so riled by his ouster that they blocked the new priest, Father Joseph Dombrowski, from celebrating Mass. When Christmas Day came a few weeks later, the angry parishioners, fueled by holiday zeal, organized a protest march to the diocesan's office that got so out of hand a twenty-four-year-old man got shot and killed by the mob.

The angry faction soon split off and followed its disgraced priest down the road, where he established a new church, Sweetest Heart of Mary, at Canfield and Russell, where it still stands today. It quickly had thousands of its own parishioners.

The two groups, so notorious around town that they earned the names Kolasinskians and Dombrovites, kept at each other's throats for years, like gangs of Old Detroit. Another altercation between the two factions on Christmas Eve 1891 led to the killing of a nineteen-year-old man.

All this because a priest was replaced at a church.

Eventually, both groups settled down in their own districts. By the turn of the century, two thousand families were attending St. Albertus, even as it shared a neighborhood with four other Polish Catholic churches. That's how densely populated Poletown was back then.

But as the parishioners started moving out of the city, the number of families belonging to St. Albertus was halved by the 1930s, and by the 1950s it was down to seven hundred. Its school closed for lack of enrollment in 1966. And once the church drew only handfuls of worshippers on Sundays, it was doomed. The last official Mass here was in 1990.

A handful of die-hards, though, begged church officials to let them keep the place. They convinced the archdiocese to sell them the entire property—church, rectory and school—for a mere $100, plus the costs of maintaining it as a museum.

"We didn't want it torn down," says Brian Baka, sixty-five, one of the three remaining original members of the group that bought it. "My dad went to school here, my parents were married here, my dad's funeral was one of the last ones here. I couldn't let it go."

STEP INSIDE ST. Albertus and it's easy to see why the church generates such devotion from its caretakers.

The outside is relatively plain, but the interior is astonishing. Color and texture and detail shine out from every direction. It's psychedelic, bizarre, otherworldly—like some mystical experience expressed

Father Edward Kaszak prepares to say Mass.

in architecture. A plaster St. Albertus looks down from above the main altar, surrounded by angels of various hierarchies floating alongside him, standing on platforms, leaning out from walls. There are flowers and candles everywhere, and little flames cast flickering shadows onto the kaleidoscope walls. The curved plaster ceilings are painted a soft blue and dotted with tiny gold stars, a fanciful depiction of the heavens beyond.

Mannequins stand near a sepulchre at the rear of the church, clothed in Polish folk costumes, clutching baskets of food, eternally heralding Easter. Large, painted sculptures of holy figures stare at you from all directions.

The most arresting displays are the altar-flanking, illuminated glass coffins containing life-size mannequins representing the corpses of St. Stanislaus and St. Hedwig, two Polish icons. They lie in stiff repose, faces pale, hands folded, eyes shut.

"It's a reminder that death is coming," Duda explains. "Be prepared however you want to be prepared—religiously, with your family, but be prepared. Death was a very important part of life in the nineteenth century because people didn't live very long, and they'd die horrible deaths from plague or broken bones or something."

The exuberant ornamentation at these old churches was meant to elevate those gathered there to a higher state of mind, to evoke a sense of holiness. It's a big reason the caretakers are so invested in St. Albertus.

"When I come here, I feel like I've been to church," Baka says. "I don't like the modern churches. None of us do. I don't feel like I've been to a church when I've been in those."

LIKE ANYTHING LEFT behind in the city, the church was soon at the mercy of the scavengers and vandals who make quick work of empty places.

Scrappers tore the old school apart. Thieves broke into the rectory. They got into the church. They even took the picnic tables from the courtyard, after taking the rainspouts. Surrounded by nothingness out here, there were no witnesses, no calls to police, nobody standing in their way.

The association had been raising money for a new boiler to keep everything from freezing, but then scrappers got on the roof and tore away some of the long copper panels. That added $12,000 to the group's bills.

The church's kaleidoscope interior glows when the sun beams through the stained-glass windows.

Children of the parishioners celebrate the city's rich Polish history at Polish Heritage Mass.

Half their efforts consist of fortifying the place against the never-ending onslaught. The other half is raising money to keep it alive.

For the past six years, supporters have organized the St. Albertus Fest, a day of bands, food and tours of the church. They also rely on donations from long-gone residents who, though they don't attend church here anymore, want to keep this last connection to their childhoods alive.

Duda, whose family came from here, whose father was born two blocks away, who spent countless Sundays praying here, is among those whose personal ties to this place fuel his passion for it. Yet beyond the spiritual reasons, for him and for others, the dazzling beauty of this old church is reason enough to save it.

"That's why we keep it going," he says. "They don't make 'em like this no more."

Banner Year

She Lived to See 106 Birthdays,
a Milestone that Didn't Go Unnoticed

THE FAMILY HUNG the banner again this year, but this time it was different.

When Virginia Spencer's relatives started doing it six years ago, it was to celebrate the noteworthy milestone of the family matriarch's century on earth.

They strung it along the second-floor iron balcony of their east side duplex, announcing to the drivers heading downtown on East Warren that Mama, as everyone called her, had made it to her 100th birthday.

That first year, Mama wasn't happy about it. "She said, 'I don't like the idea very well,' but anyway we put it up and everybody thought it was just grand," says Dorothy Ziegler, Spencer's seventy-eight-year-old daughter.

A "Happy Birthday" banner went up every summer after that for another six years, each one noting how old she was, each one signaling a further triumph over age, illness and time. This April, though, Spencer was admitted to the emergency room and never discharged, and she passed away in a hospital bed, several miles from home, in an unfamiliar room.

"She just went on away in peace," says Betty Seay, the fifty-four-year-old neighbor who wound up being Spencer's caregiver in her final years. "It was like she was just sleeping. She had on her powder blue and stuff. She was just peaceful."

As the family gathered to mourn Spencer's death, a cousin came up with the idea of one more banner, to let all of Mama's friends and well-wishers know that there wouldn't be another birthday celebration this summer. When the printer they'd used heard she died, he came to work on Sunday, his day off, just to make the final banner for the family.

Dorothy Ziegler (left) and Betty Seay with a photo of Mama.

It read, "Thank you for 106 years Granny. We will miss you."

Once it was strung up a few days after her death, friends and neighbors and strangers saw it and came by to offer their condolences. A truck from the nearby fire station pulled up and blared its siren, and the firemen, who knew Mama from taking her to the hospital over the years, got out to pay their respects.

Something about the banner drew people to her in her last years. "People would come from all over, and they'd be talking about the banner," Ziegler explains, "and my cousin said, 'It's only fair to put something up, let the people know, 'cause they have been looking for it every year. You owe that to them.'"

THE BANNER BECAME somewhat of a local cultural phenomenon over the years. People from the east side and the west side, people from the Grosse Pointes, people from as far away as Flint would make the journey to see if the banner made it up another year, thus showing that Mama had beat the odds once again. Neighbors would stop by on her birthday with presents, passersby would pull up and take pictures of the house, strangers would knock on the door and introduce themselves.

"You would be surprised," Ziegler says. "They would come by and say, 'We had to get our courage up to come up,' and I said, 'Oh, you're welcome,' and my mother would talk to them." They'd bring birthday cards and food platters, and bring their little children into the house to meet her, to show that there is hope of having more time than most people are granted.

She got congratulatory letters and plaques from Detroit mayors, from council members, from the governor herself one year.

Word spread. Ziegler once went to an appointment with her doctor, and when the receptionist heard she was from the east side, she told Ziegler that she should check out this one house on the corner of East Warren and Holcomb, where a banner hangs to celebrate the city's reportedly oldest grandmother.

"She said, 'Ms. Ziegler, you should see it. It is awesome.' And she said, 'Every year I look for it. People far and near know about it.' And I said, 'That's my mother!'"

VIRGINIA SPENCER WAS born in 1904 in Seneca, South Carolina, made stops in Atlanta and Washington, D.C., and wound up in Detroit in the mid-'60s. She was working at a dry cleaner at fourteen years old when the fingers on her right hand got caught in a machine used to press sheets, and the bones were crushed.

Some hack doctor wrapped the fingers too tight—it was the Deep South after all, and a little black girl's injuries likely didn't merit much care—and when the bandages came off, the fingers and the hand had become infected. Her arm had to be amputated up to the elbow.

Still, she learned how to drive, how to wring out a wet quilt, how to change diapers with one hand, because she refused to wear an artificial arm. She eventually got herself a truck that she used to collect bundles of paper and stacks of old cardboard and sell them for pennies to eke out a living.

"She refused any welfare help," Ziegler says. "Mama was a very independent woman, and there were times I wish she was on the welfare. Everybody else was on the welfare around us, but I understood, and she ingrained into us that dignity."

A couple of years ago she'd developed dementia and lost nearly all her sight and grew irritable. But even after she turned one hundred, she'd bake cornbread for the family, or barbecue pork chops on a grill out back, or pass the time watching *Jerry Springer*, her favorite show.

"My son and her would be up here, and she'd say, 'Eric, it's time for *Jerry*,'" Ziegler says. When Eric died of the flu a couple of years ago, Spencer used her fading mind as an excuse to tune out the world, her family believes.

"That took a lot out of her, but she kept it in," Ziegler says of her son's death. "I thought maybe she didn't understand he was dead, but I found out she did because she would talk about him to Betty when I wasn't around, but she said very little about him when I was there."

Spencer and Seay, the caretaker, grew very fond of each other in their time together. "The night before she passed she said, 'Betty, take me home.' I thought she was talking about *here* home, but she was really letting us know that she was ready to go," Seay remembers. "I think she knew then, 'cause she was just nice and peaceful."

THEY'RE STILL GETTING used to Mama's absence from the house. It takes time to break old habits, like checking in on her bedroom to make sure she's OK, cooking meals for her, letting her know her favorite TV shows are on.

"I would get up, and by the time I get to Mama's room I'd know Mama's not here, and I'd catch myself, so I'd play it off and go up to the front like I was looking out the door," Ziegler says, and then points at Ziegler. "I didn't want her to know what's going on."

The house still has Mama's fingerprints all over it. A photo of Detroit mayor Coleman Young, her favorite, still stands on a shelf, wrapped in plastic the way some elderly people wrap all sorts of things in plastic. A painting of a dark-skinned Jesus still hangs on the wall. And her old soft chair still sits in front of the television.

The family plans to re-hang the goodbye banner again this August, from the beginning of the month until August 31, Mama's birthday. Then it comes down forever.

It'll be the final nod toward a life that, like so many anonymous lives in the city, touched people in countless ways, from the firemen who came by one final time, to the printer who came in on his day off to make one last banner for her, to the strangers the family just knows will come knocking again in August, wondering where Mama is.

The family says she'll still be there in a way. "She all around us right now," Seay says. "Everywhere you look, it's Mama, it's Mama. It just feels like she's still right here, you know what I'm saying? This used to be her chair, but I can just sit in this chair, it just feels so calm, at ease. Just like she's got her arms around me."

Flower Power

A Family Florist Stays Alive Despite a Fire, Dementia and Loss

SHE UNWRAPS THE pink lilies and lays them gently on the table. With a knife she trims one stem at a time, and the discarded pieces fall to the floor.

This used to be where she and her family ate together. Now it's where she works.

Patricia Duff and her husband, Nat, spent a lifetime selling floral arrangements at Byron's Flowers on Woodward in Highland Park. Then, in March last year, their century-old business burned to the ground in the middle of the night.

They didn't even know their building was on fire until it was long over. Patricia would unplug the phone before going to bed because Nat had trouble sleeping. And so they slept through the blaze. They learned of it only when her son's friend knocked on their door in the morning and changed everyone's lives with a few words of news.

Although everything they had in Byron's was lost, Patricia was determined to somehow keep the family business alive. And so her house became a flower shop.

"If we shut down we'd lose our business, and there was no way we were gonna shut down," says Patricia, sixty-eight.

She called the phone company the day after the fire and had the store's phone number transferred to her house in Detroit's Boston-Edison neighborhood. She brought fresh flowers home from the wholesaler, put some in the fridge and put others by the window so they'd open their clenched petals when the sunlight touched them. There were customers waiting on arrangements, standing orders that knew nothing of a fire.

And, slowly, she adapted to a new life.

"We don't have the same amount of business, but we have business," she says. "And we don't have the equipment we had, but we're still able to operate. And that's the most important thing."

Wholesalers cut her a break, letting her purchase things one by one rather than in bulk like she used to. Instead of buying invoices by the box, she prints them one at a time on a home computer. Instead of ordering professional business cards, she now gets them for only $1.99 for five hundred of them if she leaves the printer's advertisement on the back of her cards. It's less than ideal, but it's better than giving up.

"We're really strapped for cash," she says. "We just try to cut corners as best as we can. It's a lot different, but it's manageable." Her kids, Nicole and Damian, help her out without taking any pay for it.

Patricia Duff inside her home flower shop.

Some of her regular customers have found her new location, directed here by a banner the family hung along the iron fence that still circles the site of the fire.

Consultations are held in the living room, the solarium is used for storage and the flowers get trimmed and arranged in the dining room.

Patricia wants to move back to the old location, into a new building. But the insurance company, she says, is dragging its heels on paying the claim until it finishes investigating the fire. Meanwhile, the city is eager to clear the charred rubble still piled on the lot. If that happens before the investigation is done, though, the insurance won't cover it, and Duff gets stuck with a demolition bill she can't possibly afford.

So she waits, works from the house, pleads with the city to wait a little longer and hangs on day by day, trying to fulfill a promise her husband made to the family.

"The whole mindset is, in the black minority community there aren't any businesses that go on to the second generation," she says. "That has always been our goal. It's the continuance that's the most important thing, surviving to the next generation. So I want to keep my husband's dream alive. That's the reason why."

She has to keep that promise by herself now because he can't do it anymore.

PATRICIA AND NAT met in the late '50s. He'd come north from Alabama and was working at a car wash. She worked at the Dairy Queen next door. They were a mixed-race couple in a time when that meant trouble.

"It was very hard," Patricia says. "We were pulled over by the police a lot for being together. We were followed sometimes. There weren't many places in public we could go to."

Nat got his start at Byron's as a delivery driver and quickly worked his way up. "My husband would deliver them but he kept looking at the arrangements," she says. "Sometimes he would take them apart and redo them so he would learn. He taught himself."

The owner grew to love him so much that when he died in 1969, his wife was left with instructions to sell the shop to Nat, his longtime, loyal employee. The Duff family has run it ever since.

Patricia believes her husband's was the first black florist shop in the Midwest, and he was one of the first minority owners to belong to FTD, the industry's largest network. It was a lonely distinction.

"We would go to FTD conventions, and he would be one of two black people there," she remembers.

They went through a lot together at the shop. There was the time robbers came in, beat the couple and threw them down the stairs, all for $200. The time when celebrants broke in and stole flowers to commemorate one of the Pistons' championships. The time a drunk drove his car right through the front wall of the shop. The time burglars broke in and rummaged through everything, all while the terrified family listened from the other room, where they had been sleeping after pulling an all-nighter before a busy holiday.

"There were a lot of things that happened at the flower shop, but we stayed," she says. "We're survivors."

Then came the fire.

HER HUSBAND DOESN'T live at home anymore. He'd recently begun to slip into dementia, and Patricia found herself taking care of him full time. The seventy-year-old man had endured four strokes and open-heart surgery and developed a host of other health problems that proved impossible for her to handle alone. Last fall, she had to move him into a nursing home.

She goes to see him every single day, sometimes twice a day. The couple spent so many years at the shop, so much time side by side, that he's still got that life ingrained in his mind, too deep to be diminished by a slipping memory. Patricia sometimes gets calls from the nursing home staff in the middle of the night because Nat's up and about, convinced it's time to go to work at his flower shop. She has to get up, get dressed, get down to the nursing home and console him back to sleep by telling him she already handled the day's orders.

"I say, 'Nat, I did it for you; you don't have to do it.' And he'll say, 'You did? That was really nice of you.' But fifteen minutes after I leave, once I settle him down and get him in bed, he doesn't even know I've been there."

Her days are busier than ever now. Besides the enduring flower business, besides the visits to her husband, she's also an artist, with her own studio in the Scarab Club in Midtown and drawings exhibited in eight shows since the first of the year. And she babysits seven grandkids most days. "So it's a nursery and a flower shop in a house," she laughs.

It's spring again, and it shows in her home. Roses jostle with water bottles for breathing space in the fridge, lilies yawn in the sunlight by the window and the air is suffused with the perfume of all the blooms that have passed through the old house. For another year now, the flower shop is being kept alive, a promise is kept to her family and a vow is kept to her husband.

"It's difficult," she says. "It's real tough. But you know, I'm a firm believer in the old school. You know—you marry, you marry for life, and you take care of each other. It could be me. And I would want him to do the same thing for me."

No Place Like Home

A West Side Folk Artist Fashions His Vision of a Dream World

THE ROAD WINDS past crowded gardens and flowering trees, past the horse barn and the pool and up to the gated mansion.

It's a beautiful place for someone to call home. The main house has sixteen rooms, a wide balcony on the second floor, plush furniture on hardwood floors and lots of space in which to wander and get lost.

This is Jother Woods's dream home. And he will never live here.

All of it—the sprawling lawns, the big house with the white columns, the evergreens and the colorful flowers—are barely a foot high.

"This is my imaginary estate," Woods says, proudly. He's eighty-one and a spindle of a man—tall and lanky with long limbs. He's dreamed of this place since he was a child growing up poor in the Louisiana countryside. And since he was never able to own such a home in real life, he created it as a piece of art.

The project, which he named "Plantation House," grew piece by piece over the course of three decades. It started with his dream house and spread outward until it became a landscape fifty-two feet long and six feet wide.

It's like nothing else. It's deep and rich and thick with details and surprises. Everything in it is made from someone else's trash, from the house and the barns down to the tiny furniture inside and the shrubs and flowers bordering the roads that bend through the plantation.

The trees are made from the branches of a plastic Christmas tree that Woods found lying in the road. The swimming pools are ice cube holders from old freezers, which he fills with water. The gates were once air conditioner grates, and knobs from kitchen faucets are turned over and made into planters that flank the mansion's doors. Its blueprints are drawn on an old roll-up shade.

Jother Woods sits in front of his dream estate.

A pool sits behind the house and the main garage.

Woods takes anyone who visits his house on a tour of it like he would an actual home, pointing out what each piece of Plantation House was before he found it discarded somewhere and made it useful again. "There's parking coming in off the highway," he notes, his finger tracing its path. "You cross the bridge, boathouses, boatyard, and then you're in the garden."

The project's so big, there's no room to keep it in one piece. For now, he's got much of it set up in his cinderblock basement, in the dark, waiting to be shown off. Several panels are detached and stacked against his basement walls or stored in upstairs bedrooms.

"The garden house is here, I put my garden tools in there and this is just for relaxing," he says of the patio. "I got beautiful outdoor furniture here. And you see the winding private road coming around."

As he talks, you can sense how this idea grew, layer by layer, in the mind of a kid born in a shack on a farm, dreaming of a better life someday.

WOODS GREW UP during the Depression in Horse Shoe Lake, Louisiana. "Nothing but cotton fields, corn and a river," he says. The family lived in an old wood house, where Woods shared a small bedroom with five snoring brothers crowded into two beds. Their father was a sharecropper.

The garbage provided most of the family's belongings. "We would just mostly search out white people's trash and throwaways, so I've been into recycling for over sixty years," he says, without sarcasm. Back then, down there, people just threw their garbage in ditches along the side of the road, he says. He and his brothers would climb down and sift through the refuse—from the better parts of their segregated town—for salvageable toys.

"Those little white kids had the trappings we never thought of, like old beat-up bikes, scooters, tricycles and little old trucks and things like that that were almost a mystery to us, you know, 'cause we were used to getting half an apple, half an orange and maybe one piece of peppermint stick. That was our Christmas most years. Not much, I tell you."

Some days, he'd walk up the road and see, off in the distance, the rambling plantations that contrasted so sharply with the tin-roof hovels he and his neighbors lived in.

"The big plantation owners, they had those big houses and all of the trees and pecan orchards and the big house way back off the road," he recalls. "I said I am going to create my version of my personal country estate, however long it takes."

His vision started humbly. "I didn't even have pencil and paper," he says. "I didn't know what that was, so I got a stick, maybe like a grapevine or something, and I would stand out in the dirt road and I would draw in the dirt." He made images of the cars that passed by and outlines of those big mansions, fantasy images of a world that was itself almost a fantasy.

He later joined two brothers who'd already moved to Detroit, got a job in a car plant, did some landscaping and some wall sign painting, all while still salvaging things. He began creating art out of the found pieces.

"I had the blessing of being born an artist," he says. "I could draw,

Woods surrounded by his found-object art creations.

that's all I knew. I would take my stick and draw this big house and this car. Finally, I said I should be able to make this."

IT ALL STARTED with a little wooden car. Woods carved his dream auto out of a solid block of wood, a blend of the era's car styles and models in his head. It was so impressive, it landed him a job.

"I got the privilege of being interviewed at Parks and Recreation to teach arts and crafts," he says. In lieu of a résumé, he gave them the hand-carved car to look over. "That was my ace in the hole, to prove my ability to teach, and that's how I got the job, that little green car."

To protect it, he built a portable container that was fashioned into a garage with a handle. Then he made a breezeway. And a sunroom. Then, he figured, what's a garage without a home attached to it?

From there he couldn't stop adding to it—gardens, pools, guest houses. It became an imaginary home, with plenty of room for everyone, where nobody would have to share a tiny bedroom with five snoring brothers.

HIS DETROIT HOME is nothing like his dream estate.

He lives in the lower flat of a west side duplex that overflows with his artwork—models of semi trucks made from stray pieces of wood,

The Plantation House, the centerpiece of Woods's art project.

An outhouse in the back is nestled in a profusely colorful garden.

a series of framed drawings of rotting sharecropper homes posted gallery style on a wall, big lamps made out of industrial scraps, a dollhouse model of the shotgun shack he grew up in and panels of his dream world stacked throughout the house, ready to be reassembled.

It's been exhibited over the years at the Southgate Civic Center, at the Somerset Mall and most prestigiously at the Charles H. Wright Museum of African American History a decade ago. He's hoping for one more big show, one that will earn him enough money to go back home for good.

He accepted long ago that he'll never live on such an estate, part of why his dream spilled into his art. Now he just wants the humid air and the long summers of the South, no matter the size of his house. After nearly a lifetime in Detroit, he still misses Louisiana.

"I still want to go back and live my life out back there," he says. "I just need the wherewithal. If I could get a long-term exhibition or sell it, I would leave tomorrow."

He looks over the whole landscape of his project, a life's dream so big no room can hold it. "But I would miss it tremendously. I love it."

Last Chance Saloon

This Could Be the Last Bar at the End of the World

THERE ARE THREE drinkers on the barstools. Here at Dyer's Bar and Grill, that's a packed house.

All three live in the apartments in this building, so this is literally their home bar. Besides, along this rough span of Gratiot Avenue between Connor and East McNichols, few strangers ever drop in anyway.

"Every now and then," says Jimmy Dyer, the forty-eight-year-old owner and bartender. "They see a bar sign and there's no bars on Gratiot, so you have somebody going to a game downtown and they're like, 'What the hell is this? We didn't know you were here.'"

Dyer's is as barebones as it gets. If you want a beer, you've got few choices. Apart from the Milwaukee's Best on tap for $1.25 a glass, there's Bud and Bud Light and Miller and Miller Lite. That's it. Cans only, for $1.75. "They're safer," Dyer jokes. "You get hit in the head with a bottle, it hurts a little more."

There's no cable or satellite on the lone TV, so viewing rotates among a handful of meager options. Today it's *Antiques Roadshow* on PBS, which the drinkers eye with a resigned weariness, the kind you get from years of watching shows you'd rather not watch. The lights are kept dim, so it's hard to see the wall rug portraying dogs playing poker, or the vintage jukebox collecting dust in a dark corner, or the out-of-tune piano people played years ago. A beam of daylight pours in through the open door at the back, shining hard on the faces of the old-timers occupying stools along the bar.

This is the world Dyer supervises, day after day. "It's pretty much not tending bar, it's taking care of the old guys," he says of his job here. "It's kind of like adult foster care, in all honesty."

The Dyers—Dylan, Debbie, Pops and Jimmy—inside their bar.

Dyer's is like the last outpost in a dying place. Bars once lined this stretch of Gratiot before their owners bailed for the suburbs and the drinkers followed.

Now this block is like an island. "We're kind of like a little pie in the middle of Detroit, like another Hamtramck or Highland Park. It's like the Wild West saloon where everybody meets up and does their thing."

The surrounding neighborhood is a mess—empty homes whose lawns have grown high after the spring rains, front-porch drug sales in plain sight and groups of unemployed men loitering on street corners during working hours.

The family planted flowers out back, and they keep their grass cut, making the property stand out. "You can actually tell when you come through, it's different here," Dyer says. He owns the whole building. The bar shares an address with a used appliance store and ten apartments he rents to an odd assortment of mostly white, mostly poor, mostly older folks, many of whom grew up in the neighborhood and are the last holdouts, relieved they don't have to wander away from their island to have a beer in a bar.

For years, the family owned a restaurant across the street, then bought this bar in the late '70s, when it was called the Snow Owl and featured German-themed decor, including personal beer steins that hung on the wall for each regular.

Back then, crowds of nearby factory workers who wanted a burger and beer filled the place every day. Those workers, and their workplaces, are now long gone. So is the grill. A few years ago, city inspectors demanded they put in an expensive ventilation system. That was the end of the meals.

It's a family bar in the truest sense. Dyer and his wife, nicknamed Snoopy, serve the drinks. Her father, known as Pops, spends his days on a stool at one end of the bar.

Their niece Debbie works here too sometimes, putting her ten-month-old son in the playpen that sits by the cooler. And the customers, usually the same faces they see going up and down the stairs to the apartments, are like family by virtue of familiarity.

Though the place hasn't turned a real profit in years, Dyer keeps the bar open year after year because almost all his customers are his tenants, and he knows they have nowhere else to go. He's become their caretaker in a way.

"I've grown up with most of these guys, so you kind of feel like, what are you going to do, shut down? These guys are pretty much all landlocked in this area anyway. Most of them don't drive. They've been around in this neighborhood probably all their life. Everybody else died, packed up or ran, and they're still here."

Tom Crunk's the exception. He's a suburbanite whose circumstances forced him to move into the inner city, the wrong way along the crowded path of migration out from Detroit. "It's a culture shock, let me tell you," he says, pouring beer from a can into his glass. "I'm starting to learn my way around, but as a norm you don't come down here."

Dyer loves to make fun of him for moving to the area.

Crunk lives in one of the ground-floor apartments. A few years ago, he was an engineer at an auto supplier in the suburbs. But the economy crumbled, and he lost his job, then his house, then his health as he underwent knee surgery, which required him to stay with someone who could help him as he recovered. His sister lives in this building, so he moved in with her last year. Thus began his introduction to inner-city neighborhood life in Detroit.

"Had a few problems, had a few discussions with people. They know not to discuss it with me anymore," the stocky fifty-four-year-old says with a menacing confidence. "I might be an old man, but I'm not a shy old man."

He's got a steel door for his apartment to make it harder for burglars to get in, but things still happen. Not long ago, he was lying on the couch when several guys from the neighborhood walked in after admiring his TV from outside.

"I left my front door open," he explains. "Don't do that."

Regardless, he's armed and ready. "If you wanna come in I'm gonna blow you right back out into Gratiot," the army vet says. "That's the one thing the army taught me—how to kill."

Actually, most trouble comes from the police, who apparently can't believe white people still live in this area, let alone operate a bar here. Everyone at the bar shares stories of being stopped, searched, followed or harassed by the cops as soon as they step away from the building.

Dyer has come to accept it as a reality of staying in this neighborhood. "It works on both sides of the line," he notes. "If you're black and you're in the suburbs you get stopped. Same thing happens here—if you're white you get stopped here, because nine out of ten white guys down here are buying drugs and they shouldn't be around. It's the same thinking, and I understand that."

Though few new faces are seen here, and there are countless hassles in this area, Dyer says he stays because he has optimism about the city's future, and his future in it, despite being in a part of town where there's little reason to be hopeful right now.

"Somewhere down the line something's got to happen good in the city," he says. "I think we've already been to the bottom stage; there's no way but up. But how far up before you realize something's happening? Other parts of the city might actually be seeing some signs, but we might be stuck in the last war zone."

Crunk finishes his beer. Pops nurses his in the shadows. And the baby rests in Dyer's arms as he sips a coffee and tends to the old-timers, and makes fun of Crunk yet again for moving to this neighborhood.

Then Crunk leans back, thinks for a second and says, in a blend of both sarcasm and sincerity, "This is the best bar in the world." And he cracks open another can of beer.

Signs of Faith

A Detroit Mother's Grief Is Transformed One Nail at a Time

WHAT CAN IT actually accomplish?

It's just a sign, stark and simple, and it declares, in the kind of religious language that saturates the city's culture, that "God said...Thou shall not kill." And suddenly it was appearing on trees and poles all over town.

The woman behind it says the idea came to her in the dead of night.

"I know when you write about the spiritual position, people don't really like to see that," Ovella Andreas says, "but I was asleep, and the spirit of God woke me up."

Andreas, forty-eight, is a former church organist who sat for years quietly by the choir until one day she felt the urge to become a pastor. Some years and a lot of training later, she has her own congregation. A few months back, she had a dream that told her to plaster the city with those posters, so at every turn there will be a challenge to the conscience of someone who might take a life.

Andreas admits that her plan is idealistic, an act of faith where nothing else has worked, an appeal to deep-down memories of Sunday sermons about right and wrong in a town where church is still woven into everyday life.

"Of course, there are people who say, 'What can a poster do? Are you serious? These guys could not care less about Thou shall not kill,'" Andreas says. "But the reality is we're losing ten or fifteen people a week to senseless death. Even though we don't know if it's going to do anything, it's better than doing nothing."

She called several printing shops, and a handful made signs for free. She told people about her idea, and some took a few to hang in their neighborhood. A movement began.

Bernice Reed (left) and Ovella Andreas at the shrine to Reed's murdered son.

If they were carpenters, they'd be boarding up empty houses. If they were cooks, they'd be feeding the hungry. But they're church people, and this is what they do.

"This is really the only thing that we have to work with from this side," Andreas says.

SOME DON'T THINK it'll accomplish much at all.

Among them is the Reverend Willie Lewis, who waits outside a church as a rally is to begin under a cloudy sky that threatens rain. The Obedient Missionary Baptist Church on the city's west side organized it, announced it, invited people to stop by and take a stand against the violence that's so much a part of city life.

Yet at the designated hour, there are but two dozen people here, seated at tables, holding stenciled posters or standing by the church steps, waiting for something to happen. Andreas's signs are stacked on a table, ready to be tacked up somewhere. It's not her event, but she was invited to speak here.

Lewis stands nearby in a dark green suit, his hair salt-and-pepper, his demeanor dignified and formal. "All the publicity and this is how it is?" he says in a gravelly voice, looking over the small group that showed up.

The seventy-four-year-old pastor walked the few blocks from his church, Meditation Missionary Baptist, because the rally's organizers asked him to be here to lend some heft to the proceedings. He shakes his head in disappointment, not just at the numbers, but also because this rally, like so many of its kind, mostly draws women who come to lament the havoc wrought by men.

"You got to look for the men and boys," he says, seeing few. "Who's that doing all the violence out there? Men. How you gonna stop that, except with men? Women aren't the ones who are gonna stop nothing. The men are doing it."

Out on the curved road that sweeps past the church, a few church kids shout at the traffic and hold up handmade placards reading, "Give peace a chance" and "Thou shall not kill." Some cars honk as they pass by.

"That's naïve," Lewis says. "I don't call it wasting time because people should do *something*, but we're like the wild, wild West. Remember the violence there? How did they stop that? Force—sheriff's department, police, law enforcement. But there's no police here today, man. The police department's in disarray."

As a church leader, he wants the same thing as these women and children do, but after decades of rallies and killings, he's come to doubt that peaceful methods like this will do anything.

But as the traffic light out front goes red, a car stops next to a kid on the side of the road.

The driver asks for a sign.

BERNICE REED LEAVES the rally for a moment and drives with Andreas to a curbside memorial a mile or so away.

It was just someone's tree until Reed's son got shot next to it. Then his friends and family tied stuffed animals and pictures to it, and now that homeowner has a shrine to a dead kid in his front yard.

When Reed pulls up and sees it, she begins to cry. It's been more than a year since her son was murdered, yet she's never been here before. The sight of this tree cuts through a year's worth of defenses and brings it all back.

What's worse, he was the second of her two sons murdered. The oldest was killed ten years ago at age twenty-five. Shot by someone he knew, Reed says, after a fistfight escalated. Her youngest was shot in March last year. He made fun of a friend and the friend didn't like it. "The guy who killed my baby boy said he played too much," the fifty-three-year-old says. "He'd play with you until he aggravated you, so that's why he killed him." Both died on the same street, Meyers, a decade apart. Reed had been to one son's memorial but not this one.

"For some reason, with my older son, I would go there all the time and put balloons up, and I would go to the cemetery, but I think by this being my baby at eighteen years old, I don't know how to explain it."

Not long ago, Reed heard Andreas on the radio talking about the campaign, called in for signs and started driving around town and leaving them everywhere. If she hears on the news that someone's been killed, she drives to that spot and posts a sign. If she sees a telephone pole or a tree with stuffed animals attached, she'll leave a sign there too.

The poster campaign makes perfect sense to her. "Most people are raised up in church," she reasons. "Even if they stray away, they're brought up in church, so when you see the word 'God,' a lot of people fear the name, if they don't fear anyone else. Somebody might see the posters and think twice."

Being face to face with the memorial makes the memories tumble out: how she taught her son to save his money, taught him how to work for what he wanted in life, taught him how to be a man. Memories that drive her to put up these posters.

"Whatever I can get them to nail into," Reed says. A tree. A telephone pole. Anything.

But what can it actually accomplish?

Reed will tell you that, if nothing else, if nobody is moved by her efforts, if nothing changes, it still keeps her from falling to pieces. It channels the grief. It's an outlet for an anguished mother's helplessness and pain. Something good has to come out of those deaths, otherwise they would be truly meaningless.

"I don't want another mother to go through what I went through," Reed says.

After lingering a little while, Reed and Andreas climb back into the car and drive away from the shrine. There's a rally to return to and signs to be hung.

Graveyard Shifts

An East Side Headstone Store with a Heart

FOUR PEOPLE WITH grim faces walk into the tombstone store.

They've come here, to Otto Schemansky Sons Monuments on Van Dyke near McNichols, to get a marker for the grave site of a seven-year-old girl shot and killed by Detroit police in a bungled raid several weeks back. These four, a mess of street manners and empty pockets, are her family.

After all the news stories and press conferences, and the candles and stuffed animals stacked on their front porch, they're still burdened with the lonely duty of buying a headstone for a dead little girl.

They've come because this place supplied a grave marker for a Detroit toddler who died not too long ago when the car she was riding in ran a stop sign and plowed into a van, throwing her out the window. That family had no money for a headstone, so store owners Paul and Mary Weeks donated one to them. Word spread, as these things do through the neighborhoods, and now another family too broke to buy a decent gravestone found their way here.

Paul slowly takes the time to show them the options, such as the different lettering that's available. "The gold letters really pop," he tells them. "Won't cost any extra," he adds.

"How much?" mumbles the girl's father, wearing cornrows and a white T-shirt. He's doing all the talking for the family.

Normal price for the lettering is about $225. Paul looks at him, thinks it over. "One-fifty," he says. The father says they'll talk it over and come back later.

Many customers here can't afford elaborate monuments for their deceased loved ones. Others can't buy a marker at all, so someone they cared about winds up an anonymous bump in the cemetery grass or an urn of powder on a shelf.

You can't have no marker, though, Paul always insists, so he finds himself whittling down prices for those who show up, grieving and broke, at the business's doorstep.

"I'll tell you something," Paul says. "If you do something good like that for 'em, they'll be the first ones here to help you out if you have a problem. They remember who helps them out, who walks on them. You gotta remember that."

IT'S A TOUGH business when every one of your customers comes to you in misery.

"Selling this is not like selling anything else," Mary says. "It's a once-in-a-lifetime purchase. I know a lot of times I have a family in and they can't make up their mind, and they'll say, 'Oh, I'm sorry,' and I tell them, 'Don't be sorry. You're going to do this only one time for them.'"

Mary's family purchased Otto Schemansky Sons Monuments in 1977 from the great-grandchildren of its founder and namesake, who started the business in 1883 on lower Gratiot near downtown. It migrated north and over to Van Dyke in the mid-1940s, into a square cinderblock building with a workshop out back. When Mary's dad bought it, he kept its century-old name instead of putting his own up on the sign. After he retired, Mary and Paul took over.

There used to be more than a dozen monument engravers along this strip of Van Dyke, which runs between several of the city's old cemeteries. Now there are only two stores left. This one's the oldest.

Mary, fifty-seven, handles the office work; husband Paul, forty-three, their kids and Mary's brother do the heavy lifting outside. They've all learned to deal gently with distraught customers, though Mary is the most soothing and comforting and the first person a customer sees. Sometimes she finds herself hugging the more distraught mourners who come through the door. Most are from this wrecked east side neighborhood.

"I love them," she says. "It's a different world down here. It makes you appreciate what you have. You feel for them. They have a real struggle, and they're good people."

Payment plans are available, but all monuments have to be paid in full before they're placed in the cemetery. Once they're in the ground, they can't be repossessed because that would violate state grave-robbing laws.

The markers are granite and come in different colors, shipped from different quarries around the world. Prices range from $200 for a small slab with a name and dates on it to $30,000 and more for tall sculptures to as much as hundreds of thousands for a private mausoleum. No matter what, Paul is adamant that something—anything—should be on someone's grave.

"You can't just have nothing there!" he says, volume rising. "To me, whenever I see something with nothing on it, it tells me the family never respected them."

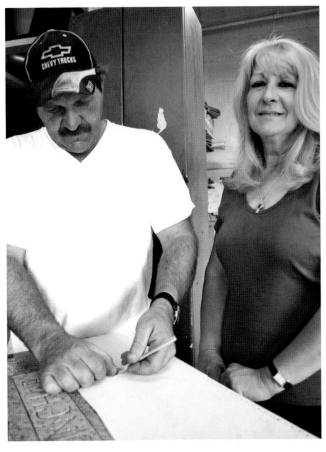

Paul and Mary Weeks in their tombstone store's workshop.

THERE'S AN OLD house next door, shuttered and empty. A man named James lived there for years; after Paul began working down here, the two grew close. "One of my best friends," Paul says. "He taught me so much about Detroit." One day the family realized they hadn't seen James in a while. Paul broke into the house and found him lying there, dead. "He didn't take care of himself," Paul explains.

After that, the Weeks family tended to James's old, blind dog until he, too, died. They buried him in the yard, under the spot where he liked to lie.

The lawn grew wild and the family kept cutting it. Thieves would try to break in, and Paul would scare them off.

Pretty soon, Paul—stocky, thick-armed and quick-tempered—found himself chasing away people trying to get into other houses or cars. Neighbors noticed and started calling him to report crimes in progress. "Whether it's Mandy or Dave down the street or whoever, they'll call down here when they see somebody messing around by one of these houses 'cause they know—*boom*—I'm gone," he says, shouting. When Paul gets worked up, his face becomes flushed and menacing. "I'll go right out after them, damn right, and everybody's yelling at me—'Hey wait a minute, you forgot your gun.' I don't care."

Paul moved to the Detroit area from a little town up north years ago and married his best friend's sister in the 1980s. After all this time working in the city, it's gotten into his veins, grown to fascinate him. For a while he was trying to buy James's house to stay in during the week, to spend the night and live through what his neighbors live through, like the woman who tells him of nights spent lying on the floor with her two kids when shootouts happen out in the street.

"What gives me a right to have a business in this community if I'm not part of the community?" he says.

So he chases thieves, and mows lawns, and gives out food baskets during holidays. He's part of a group that renovated nearby Fletcher Field, installing playground equipment and keeping the weeds cut. He basically adopted himself into the neighborhood, a self-designated caretaker for the old ladies and little kids and the helpless—pretty much anyone who seems trapped or lost out here in this wild, sometimes dangerous neighborhood.

"The ones who are stuck down here, there are some good people," Paul says, standing in the store's fenced-in yard. Two guard dogs at his feet glare at strangers passing by. "You'll meet some wonderful people around here that I like better than even my own family members. They're a lot better people. But they're just caught."

Down on the Corner

One Man's Grill Is Another Man's Hangout

HIS BARBECUE STAND is stocked with two grills, a hot dog cart and a group of men who seat themselves at his side every day.

Charles Gaither can be found on the corner of East McNichols and Hoover six days a week, from just before lunch until the sun sinks away, standing over two barrel grills that bathe him in heat and smoke. This is how he supports himself and his four kids.

Gaither's one of countless grillers in the city who station themselves on sidewalks and parking lots during summertime, selling barbecued meat for a few dollars a meal. But while many do so as a side job to a main business like a barbershop or a party store, Gaither relies on this alone to pay his bills. It makes for long days of work at the mercy of the weather.

"It's about two or three hours before I get here of preparation—loading the truck up, getting things set up, making sure things are ready to go," says the tall, thin thirty-eight-year-old. "And it's about two or three hours after I leave here—take everything off the truck, gotta wash the dishes, then I'm always doing something to get ready for tomorrow."

He calls his business "C" Chef BBQ. It's posted just like that on a framed, laminated menu that rests on the folding table where customers stand and order their food and on a hand-painted sign propped near the sidewalk. The parking lot he works in belongs to the church he attends. They let him set up here, under a little canopy.

Besides the usual grilled ribs and sausages, Gaither's created some unique dishes, like a leg quarter of jerk chicken on wheat bread for $4.00, Steak-umm sandwiches with onions and cheese for the same price or $1.25 hot dogs

"C" Chef Charles Gaither makes lunch for a customer.

covered in cinnamon-spiced, sweet baked beans on a bun. Drinks like red pop or lemonade go for a buck apiece.

After years of cooking in other people's restaurants, he resolved a few years ago to start one of his own.

"Nothing's easy," he says. "That I have learned the hard way. It's easier to work for somebody else because here, everything's my fault. At the end of the day, there's nobody to be mad at but me. But it's mine."

DON WILLIAMS CRACKS open a tall can of beer in a brown paper bag as he watches the passing cars. "This is one place where you can see everything happening," says the fifty-four-year-old. He's sitting next to the "C" Chef canopy with pal Earl Hodges, sixty-three, and Gaither's thirty-eight-year-old brother, Anthony.

When Gaither first opened up here, these neighborhood guys would order food and make small talk with him. Later, they brought chairs so they could hang around a while and make a day of it. Eventually, they got so comfortable they set up their own horseshoes pit on the long strip of crabgrass between the sidewalk and the street.

People make hangouts out of all sorts of places. Porch stoops, dive bars, front lawns, city parks. For whatever reason, the soft-spoken chef, so polite that almost every sentence of his contains a "yes sir" or "yes ma'am," found himself the center around which this small group's social life orbits. His workplace became their full-time hangout.

"There's a lot of entertainment here," Williams says, leaning back in his chair. "Pretty ladies go by, everybody rides by, the bus stops right here, picks up, empties off, bus stop over there, officers night-sticking motherfuckers," he laughs. "We have a ball over here, man."

Williams is the group's talker, the one with the contagious laugh, the one always cracking jokes.

"He do not hush," the chef says about him. "God bless him, but he do not hush."

Williams, like Hodges, has been in the neighborhood for years. "I've been living here since '76. The neighborhood over here, wasn't nothin' over here black but a shoe and a tire." They all laugh. "I'm telling you the truth. Matter of fact, we was one of the first black families to move over here."

After three decades working robotics at Chrysler's Sterling Heights plant, he retired a few years ago. "It's been three years of heaven," he says. "I've never been able to sit out here like this 'cause I always worked afternoons and they'd keep me there, what, ten, twelve hours. But now I ride my bicycle up here, sit up here a couple hours when he starts up in the morning, drink a beer. That's what I like to do."

They're out here even on the short, gray days of winter, sitting close to the hot barbecue pits, sometimes taking swigs of Yukon Jack to keep warm. "Winter's very challenging," Anthony Gaither says, understated. It doesn't stop their gatherings, though.

You can tell these guys admire the chef, truly like him, even feel protective toward him. Hodges and Williams call themselves his adoptive uncles. And with his brother Anthony joining them most days when he's not working at the gas station up the street, the assembled group has the relaxed familiarity of relatives sitting around the yard.

"It's a family thing," says Hodges. "We stay up here until eight o'clock or so some nights, and while he's loading up we stand around talking, drink a beer, you know? We hate to even leave each other 'cause this is just what we do. We stay here all day. And when someone is not here one particular day, the whole day, we wonder where they are."

CLANG! THE HORSESHOE hits the stake and falls off to the side.

"You ready for this ass whooping?" Williams says to Hodges. "Don't take it personal, though," he adds with a chuckle. He throws a second one. It bounces off the dry dirt and kicks up a whiff of dust. He's already way in the lead.

"Aw, he's just lucky right now," Hodges counters. But the score is an afterthought. Horseshoes is just another reason for these friends to stick around, something to do between bouts of sitting.

"It's a beautiful game," he says.

Anthony Gaither likes its low-exertion pace. "I'm not really a sports person, like baseball, running around and all that. I don't really want to do all that running and stuff," he says, rubbing his belly. "Just stand here and let the stomach grow a little more."

Kids ride by sometimes and ask to be taught how to play. Others come to watch. Rarely, a hustler might show up and want to join in, and before you know it they're swearing and getting riled up and trying to bet on throws. That ends the game.

As they take turns throwing and talking and throwing again, cars pull up, drivers amble out and Charles the chef hustles between his grills. Sometimes half a dozen cars will be parked around the canopy in the lot, angled in all directions, their stereos blaring, their drivers hungry. The horseshoe guys will wait for everyone to get served and invite the chef to play a quick round. He rarely has the time for it and doesn't get to hang out much, but he's still the center of this group and its reason for being here.

And the chef is perceptive enough to know this, thoughtful enough to appreciate the gesture of these guys showing up one day and adopting him and his spot as their own.

"Some days are better than others, but the relationships and the people I've met are more important than the money. I love the customers, and the people I meet out here, and these guys out here," he says, as his friends stand around joking by the horseshoe pit. "It makes it difficult to come off this corner."

Earl Hodges, Don Williams and Anthony Gaither before another game of horseshoes.

Nothin' but a G-String

Jay Thunderbolt Boasts His Very Own Strip Club—in His House

THERE'S NO STAGE at this strip club. No pole. Not even a bar. And the music comes from a boombox.

Welcome to Club Thunderbolt, the strangest place in the city to get a lap dance. It's located in the back room of an old house in an east side neighborhood of working-class bungalows.

"Everybody in the neighborhood knows what I do," says Jay Thunderbolt, the forty-five-year-old club owner, homeowner, house mom and house DJ. "In the summertime you got all these girls leaving wearing four ounces of clothing, so they kind of get what's going on."

Thunderbolt, who stopped using his real name years ago, is a striking sight. He's six-foot-five, has longish hair combed back and wears a black suit with a bulletproof vest underneath and a gun on his waist. His face droops on one side, the aftereffects of getting shot in the head in a Detroit alley when he was eleven years old.

"Before they [strippers and patrons] come over I tell everyone I'm real scary looking, so don't freak out," he says. Get past his looks, though, and he's droll and laidback, with an acute sense of the club's absurdity.

Other than the girls, he's the only one who works here. "I play everything— daddy, uncle, banker, provider of tanning," he says. His empire is called Thunderbolt Entertainment, the umbrella name of the in-house and mobile stripper service. Twenty-four hours a day, any day, you can come to a show or a show can be brought to you. He says he's open for business twenty-four hours a day and will wake up at any hour to get the club going.

Thunderbolt in the family room, which doubles as the girls' changing area.

There's no cover charge. Customers can order different strippers out of the company catalogue—a photo album full of seedy-looking Polaroids. Each page features one of his strippers in three poses—bent over, spread eagle and come hither. There are dozens of girls to choose from.

Thunderbolt doesn't need a cabaret license like other Detroit strip clubs must have. The city ordinance regulating other places doesn't apply because it's not a bar serving liquor or food but rather a private arrangement in a private home. To him, it's like having a strip-o-gram sent to your house.

"As far as I'm concerned," Thunderbolt says, "when a guy calls up to come here, he's my 'friend.'" And though the club is dry, people can still drink. "If they want to party and bring their own party favors, that's OK," he says.

There's absolutely no prostitution allowed. Thunderbolt stays in the room the whole time, watching. He takes 10 percent of the girls' earnings for his services.

His business card is vague, like a secret pass to some hidden afterhours spot. It says simply "Thunderbolt—Party Naked" next to a phone number. He

Jay Thunderbolt and Summer inside his living room strip club.

places ads now and then in newspaper classified sections offering just as few details: "Private strip club. By appointment."

The club's main room, at the back of the house, looks like a Northern Michigan lodge decorated in the 1970s. The walls are fake wood paneling. The aged carpet is greenish-brown. The seating is an old, thick sectional couch. A single bed rests suggestively in a corner. An ancient stereo receiver and eight-track tape player sit on a table. A few shotgun shells are lined up along its edge, incongruously. A patron's first visit is an eye-opener. "Usually everybody is shocked," Thunderbolt says, "but I've been in AmVet halls smaller than this."

Before every night's show, customers are given the same introduction. "Listen up," Thunderbolt announces to the room. "These are the rules: There's no licking, sticking, biting or slapping. Can't hurt the girls, gentlemen. Be good to the girls, they'll be good to you. It's ten dollars a dance with the g-string on, twenty dollars with the g-string off. OK? It's lap dance time."

THE CLUB GOT its start after a botched bachelor party. The guy across the street was getting married. Thunderbolt hired a stripper and threw him a party that went sour.

"For 225 bucks she came out, did three songs and fucking left. And I was pissed, 'cause I set it up and then it falls on me. So I said screw it, I'm gonna do this." He came up with his showbiz name, printed some business cards, hired a few strippers and began what might be the strangest home business in town.

He has had the club in several different houses, mostly on the east side. Every time he moves to a new one, he goes door-to-door to explain what's coming to the neighborhood.

"I tell everybody, 'This is what I'm gonna do. Don't be freakin' out.' I have to because the girls put a shitload of cars on the street, but I keep the grass cut, I pay the bills."

His current home belonged to his parents, who both died recently. Until a few years ago, his elderly dad shared the house with Thunderbolt and his business. His last days were spent among strippers roaming the house. "My old man didn't give a shit," he says. "There's a bunch of naked girls laying around here? Believe me, he didn't care."

Everything about Club Thunderbolt is surreal. The front room has several tall mirrors lined up against the walls, behind the easy chairs. The curtains are drawn tight. Ashtrays overflow with stubbed-out cigarettes. The walls are yellowed from years of smoking. It's dark, dank and creepy.

"It was a little weird at first," says Summer the stripper. She's twenty-nine and works at a local strip club when she's not here. A friend introduced her to the place. Now she's a regular. "I got used to it."

Weirdest of all are the framed certificates on the wall from the Republican Congressional Committee's Business Advisory Council, naming Thunderbolt as an honorary co-chair and lauding his business acumen. One is signed by Newt Gingrich, the other by Tom DeLay.

He thinks they're tied to a breast cancer fundraiser he attends and donates to. "I make my money off of boobs, so the breast cancer thing, coughing up a couple bucks seemed like good karma to me," he says. "So I happened to go to their breast cancer thing. I got invited, and for some odd reason they put me at a table with a bunch of Republicans. I never sent them a dime, but they sure do like to send me shit."

THUNDERBOLT JUST MIGHT be indestructible. As a kid, he got ten operations during a ten-month hospital stay after getting shot by a stranger as he headed home one night. He spent most of his career as a bodyguard—once for a dirty cop, another time for the owner of a porno theater. In his time, he's been stabbed with a crochet needle in the thigh. Shot in the shoulder. Stabbed in the back. Blasted by buckshot. Wounded by a bullet in his calf.

He figured that, if anything, strip club work would be less dangerous. So far so good, except for a burglary last year. The club's front door is half plywood right now because Thunderbolt nailed it there to cover the jagged hole left by the shotgun blast he aimed at the fleeing robbers. The cops showed up, took the report and scratched their heads at the mirrors and curling irons and hairspray cans everywhere. "They're looking around—'What do you do, man?'" he remembers them saying.

By now though, most cops know him and what he does. If they pass by, he'll send a welcome committee out. "I say, 'Somebody show them some boobs, press them up against the window and say thank you for being a cop,'" he says.

So cops leave him alone, as does the city. Now he's just got to attract more customers. "I imagine some time and some advertising will do it," he says. He thinks the house's advantages over traditional gentleman's clubs will outweigh the weirdness of getting a lap dance in some stranger's back room.

"I think people get tired of the minute and fifty-four seconds' worth of song," he says of normal strip clubs. At Club Thunderbolt, on the other hand, it's a flat fee that gets you long songs with no last-minute surprises. "Here, when you buy a Cadilac," he says, "you actually get rims and tires too."

The Hard Luck Café

Downtown Coffee Shop Gives the Homeless a Place of Their Own

THE SMELL INSIDE the Canticle Café is unmistakable.

It's an odor that clings to the homeless, one of long days spent out in the weather, of dried sweat and unwashed dirt.

It gets them kicked out of most places, keeps people at a distance and relegates them to a handful of spots like shelters, soup kitchens and churches, where they keep company with one another in a world within ours but separate from it.

Brother Al Mascia, a Franciscan friar with St. Aloysius Catholic Church, wanted to give the homeless an opportunity to feel what it's like to be treated as a normal person, to be served instead of being told to leave.

So a few years ago, he converted his church's warming center at Washington and State, where for years the homeless have come to escape the cold, into a traditional coffee shop for people living on the streets.

"Folks used to come in and would just serve themselves from a pot of coffee and a box of doughnuts," says Mascia, fifty-five. "We had folding chairs and a little TV with rabbit ears, and I figured we can do better than that."

They began offering poetry slams, a piano to play, computers with Internet access, a television with a DVD player, different blends of organic coffee, light food like oatmeal and sandwiches and a bakery making fresh muffins and rolls.

Same as a normal coffee shop, except here everything is free, nearly everybody is homeless and nobody gets kicked out for how they look or smell.

In fact, the patrons are called "guests" by the staff instead of "clients" and are now served coffee by volunteer baristas. "We call them 'guests' because what we're trying to do is stimulate the person's sense of self-esteem and dignity," Mascia says. They also offer traditional social services like counseling, visits with a nurse, utility assistance and warm clothing.

The café, named after a St. Francis song ("The Canticle of the Sun"), faces challenges a normal coffee shop doesn't deal with, to say the least. The air carries a sharp odor that stays in your nostrils even after you leave. The language is sometimes foul; other times it's incoherent. Some guests are crazy or strung out. A few nod out in their chairs after eating.

But most of the homeless here are well behaved and courteous, as if to live up to the dignity the café tries to foster. An orderly line forms for coffee and muffins in the morning. The audience listens politely when someone reads a poem or sings a song. And almost everyone demurs when Mascia, in the brown robe of a friar, walks by and says hello in the morning.

The café invites others from the area too, like lonely seniors who live in the high-rise, low-income apartments up and down Washington Boulevard, even downtown officeworkers. Mascia says he wants to mix people from different backgrounds, for the poor to interact with the more fortunate, for those who have it good to meet those who don't.

"Once you make friends with folks who are living on the streets, as we have here, then you can't just dismiss it, objectify it, depersonalize it," he says. "Then they become real human beings, and you become concerned for their welfare."

"WELCOME TO MY mind. Welcome to my madness."

So begins the weekly Friday morning poetry slam. Its host, Grant Chapman, is reading from a binder of his laminated poems. He stands at a podium with a primitive beat box and a microphone rigged up to crude little computer speakers, reading his poetry to a fuzzed-out beat. He's forty-eight, lives in Hart Plaza and calls himself a "soul poet."

Once he gets things rolling, audience members can come up, one by one, and say pretty much anything they want. Or sing. Or rant. There are few rules.

"Some guys will talk about their experiences on the street, sometimes they might do a freestyle rap thing, so it's pretty interesting," says Michael Thomas, the café's forty-four-year-old case manager. "It's always something a little bit different."

A woman meekly steps up to the microphone. "I've done things," she says, mysteriously, as a bare-bones beat plays behind her words. She's bundled in a coat and a wool hat. Her tone is confessional. "And I'm a sinner too. I'm not perfect." When she's finished, she thanks God for keeping her alive and asks for a round of applause for him. The room obliges.

The religious overtones of the place, like the sight of a friar wandering around, like the colorful mural of St. Francis on the wall, an idyllic scene into which the faces of some volunteers have been painted, influence some of the stream-of-consciousness performances.

Cue Fred Thompson. He stands and launches into a spontaneous religious sermon at bone-rattling volume that has the guests frozen nervously in their chairs. "He does this once a week," Chapman says, smirking. It's just Thompson's form of poetry.

Mascia never knows what talents lie hidden beneath the ragged appearance of those in the crowd. For instance, a homeless teen once came in for a doughnut. "I didn't know who he was; he didn't say a word. I thought he could be a gang member, he could be anything." Then he sat at the piano and played Pachelbel's Canon in D from memory.

"It just blew me away. You can never assume anything when it comes to the folks that we deal with. Unfortunately, many people have assumptions that lead them to be surprised that there are these many levels of richness in character and being among the homeless."

An anonymous homeless poet speaks at the weekly poetry slam.

Brother Al Mascia inside the Canticle Café.

Many of the volunteers here were once patrons. John Pokorney, who runs the bakery, lived in a fleabag motel down the street, near death and nearly homeless, spending his nights drinking away the depression that followed two bouts with brain cancer.

"I was very down and out, and one of my friends told me about this place, and I came by to get food," the thirty-one-year-old says. One side of his shorn head has a thick scar from his surgeries. When he speaks, his face shows the intensity of someone who has twice stood on the edge of death and isn't sure he's back. He still needs treatments, fistfuls of pills, endless tests and checkups.

But he asked to work here, quit drinking and stayed. "I found my purpose here."

THERE'S A NEW, landscaped boulevard running down the middle of Washington. The restored, historic Book-Cadillac hotel gleams across the street. And groups of homeless people spill out from the café, loitering in groups by parked cars or the flower beds, or ambling past out-of-towners walking down the block.

It wasn't what many had in mind when restoring this part of town.

"Some of our guests are rough around the edges, and they'll approach people, panhandling with a level of aggression that we're not happy with," Mascia says.

Since the hotel reopened and the street was redone, he's heard calls to move the café somewhere, anywhere. Just not here. Wandering vagrants and timid tourists don't mix.

The café volunteers, though, defend the homeless customers. "Very few actually panhandle right here," Thomas says. "But you're in downtown

The line of the homeless leads out the door on busy mornings at the Canticle Café.

Detroit; if you're near here and they have a problem with a homeless person, they're going to put it on us even if it's someone that I've never seen here before."

Mascia wants to keep the café in this spot downtown, because its customers call this area home. There's room here, he says, for those from the extremes of society to share the same part of the city, to give people the chance to learn something from others who live in a world very much unlike their own.

"Another way of looking at urban renewal is mixing people up, having a neighborhood of diversity," he says. "The benefit of that is the enrichment of lives all around. We're all enriched when we get to know people from different walks of life."

Bird's Eye

How an East Side Artist Brings Life to Dead Buildings

THE PLACE WAS a dump. It had been the office of a used car lot that was left to the weeds years ago, fodder for a bulldozer if anything were ever to replace it.

So a fellow named Bird came by one day with a few brushes and some cans of paint and put two paintings here; one on this ugly shack and another on the empty building next to it, both of which he had to look at every day as he walked past.

One is a portrait of Barack Obama, looking skyward. The other is an image of Michael Jackson, dancing under a spotlight. Both are figures revered out here for different reasons, captured in fine art portrayals on unexpected canvases.

The artist carefully chose this spot. "If the building has potential and I think maybe in the future they might open it up or someone might rent it, I don't bother," says Lee Walker, the fifty-two-year-old known around town simply as Bird the painter. "It has to be dilapidated—roof gone, no doors, basically abandoned."

Walker lives and works near that weathered shack, at Gratiot near Burns, in one of the city's most battered areas—far outside downtown, deep inside the inner city, a maze of beaten-up old homes on crisscrossing side streets in what has become Detroit's hinterlands.

Like other artists who use the city's empty buildings to create art, Walker has done paintings like this before, but the buildings were either torn down or fell in on themselves, and with them went his art. It hasn't stopped him from doing others.

"If I don't see no future for the structure I'll try to put some artwork up there that beautifies it. It's like when you see an old abandoned building, you

Inside the building, a painting of Moses shares floor space with old, used mattresses.

think about the decay of the city, how many people left; you know, the sad part of it. But if there's some art on it that catches your eye and it's a nice piece, it kind of lifts your spirits."

WALKER'S ART STUDIO sits in an unlit, discount mattress shop on Van Dyke called the Mattress Station, which he runs with a dozen friends and cousins who let him use it as his gallery. In good weather, his paintings lean against the front of the building, sharing space with used mattresses. When it starts

The paintings displayed outside bring a burst of color to Van Dyke.

raining, the whole crew scrambles to get them and the mattresses inside before they get too wet.

"The ones I try to sell up here, I try to make them as cheap as possible," he notes, "'cause cheap people come up here, so I'm not going to invest $250 doing a portrait that I can't get but $75 for it."

By cheap he means broke. Their store sells used box springs and mattresses to people so poor they have little choice but to sleep on someone else's discarded bed. "It's basically 'cause people in the neighborhood can't afford Gardner-White," Walker says, referring to the local furniture chain.

When business is slow, he sits out front, painting in the sunshine. When things pick up, "like the first part of the month, when everybody gets government checks or whatever," he pitches in, putting mattresses in the back of someone's truck or else delivering them if the buyer has no vehicle.

His makeshift studio provides not only space but art supplies too. Most of his paintings are done on bedsheets or on the cloth of a mattress, with part of the wood frame left in place to keep the material taut after the springs have been removed. "I've cornered the market on canvases," he jokes. "I've learned to make my own canvases cheap." Out here, you have to use what you can get.

Sometimes people driving by see his work and stop to purchase something. Framed paintings of cartoon characters are the most popular out here, though he strives to balance those with more serious pieces, like the one near the front door showing a little kid staring at a pile of guns.

"He's trying to pick the right one for a drive-by," Walker says. It's similar to another one he's working on that shows a toddler on a Big Wheel, riding with a pistol.

Guns have found their way into his work a lot lately. "A few people in my family got killed by guns," he explains. "I'd like to start some kind of nonprofit organization to do artwork on these abandoned buildings and promote nonviolence. I want to try to save some of the black kids—well, white kids too—but in my neighborhood they're killing each other with these guns every day."

Walker learned the art from his grandfather, a house and sign painter who taught him as a young child. "He used to *make* us paint," he says. "We'd get our ass whooped if we didn't paint, 'cause he knew that along further in life that we would need what he knew. And he was right."

Walker passed the skill on to his own kids, who showed an inclination to paint early on, like the time they painted everything in their new house—carpets, cabinets,

Bird at the front of the mattress store, working on his painting about the prevalence of guns in city life.

Opposite, top: Lee Walker, aka Bird, in the doorway of his Mattress Station art studio.
Opposite, bottom: Michael Jackson immortalized by Bird on Gratiot.

fish tank—with flat white latex as their parents slept after a housewarming party. "I couldn't even get mad at them," he says, smiling, "'cause I seen what they were trying to do. It's in their blood."

He hopes his work will appear in a real gallery someday, as it did a few times many years back, though most of his old pieces were lost when his Detroit house burned to the ground long ago. Until then, his paintings are on display at the makeshift studio on Van Dyke, sharing space with the mattresses leaning against the plaster walls.

"My gallery is basically out here on the streets," he says, sitting on a bucket as he brushes paint onto a stretched bedsheet. "Everybody can see you working, compared to sitting in a building, waiting for people to come in. There's a lot of opportunity here on the streets."

Band of Brothers

Vietnam Vets Create a Sanctuary in the City

AFTER MIKE SAND returned home from Vietnam in the early '70s, his dad took him to the local VFW Post. The old man had been a commander in World War II, and now that his son had served overseas, it was time to join the other vets at the hall.

"When I came home, my dad, you know—'You gotta come in and jump into all this stuff,'" Sand recalls. He found a room full of grizzled old guys, "with their Eisenhower jackets and their brush haircuts," who didn't like this kid with the shaggy hair and the long beard, looking like all the other damn hippies out there.

"Some of the World War II guys were like, 'You've got to clean up your act,' and I just wanted to get on with my life. I didn't feel like I was accepted there."

Sand is an original member of Detroit's Vietnam Veterans of America Chapter Nine, founded for guys like him coming home to welcomes like that.

"Basically, you came home and they said hide your uniform, conform with what's going on, don't have short hair, don't look like a veteran or anything, 'cause veterans aren't very popular," Sand says. The war proved as unpopular with the older vets as it was with the public. "We weren't accepted by the traditional veterans organizations because we didn't fight in a 'real' war."

For many of his fellow soldiers, being home wasn't going so well in other ways either. "You have the dreams and all that when you come back," says Jack Lynch, sixty-eight, a Chapter Nine member since the beginning. "You wake up in the middle of the night in sweats."

That kind of complaint used to be common around here. "PTSD is a terrible thing," Sand says. "In extreme cases there's so much guilt the guy just self-destructs. We've had twice as many Vietnam vets commit suicide since the war as died over there."

To this day, Steve McDonald's family wakes him up from a distance with a broomstick. "You touch me when I'm sleeping, I'll try to choke you," says the sixty-two-year-old, chuckling. He's another early Chapter Nine member. "I got post-traumatic stress. It's funny—if the TV's blasting and the grandkids are bouncing off me, I sleep like a baby, but as soon as it gets quiet, I sit right up."

When they first got home, these guys, like many other veterans, didn't want anything to do with their fellow vets, didn't want to talk about where they'd been or remember what they'd seen. But they were having problems that, it seemed, only other Vietnam vets understood.

So a few of them started getting together, reluctantly.

"The first meetings we had were, 'Where did you serve? Who were you with? I'm a bigger hero than you,' all that kind of guy stuff," Sand says. "But then we'd see a guy that really needed some help and we'd focus on that guy, and then we just started bringing them in."

Guys brought friends. Word spread. If they saw a car with the "Vietnam Vet and Proud of It" bumper sticker making the rounds back then, they'd chase the driver down and invite him to join.

The group became the Vietnam Veterans of Michigan, eventually merging with the Vietnam Veterans of America. They found an abandoned restaurant on Woodward at Temple without power or water, bought it in the late '70s with money from fundraisers and planned to make it their headquarters.

The spot seemed ideal; many Vietnam veterans had gravitated to the Cass Corridor and its cheap housing. The vets had made a local dive bar, the Old Miami, their hangout, filling it with memorabilia they brought back from the war. "You couldn't even get a seat in the Miami back then," McDonald says. The new building would give the vets another place to get together, a better spot than a bar to talk about their experiences.

McDonald was one of them. He grew up in the Corridor, went overseas, came back and wound up living for two years in a car in an alley on the same block as his childhood home. "Probably living down here was worse than 'Nam," he says, only half joking. "At least you could shoot back over there."

TAKING HOLD OF their new building was a battle in itself. The floors were knee-high with trash from the junkies and homeless who were nesting there. The basement was full of fetid water that had a dozen dead cats floating in it. The

vets kicked out the squatters, drained the muck, hauled out the trash, put a new façade on the building.

The former inhabitants, though, wouldn't go away without a fight. "We had a guy in the building, Crazy Phil, for about a year with a 9 mm and a shotgun, trying to keep the people from trying to break in," Sand says. Still, someone fired thirteen shots at the back door.

Even after they threw them out of the building, the derelicts still hung around the periphery. "Heroin addicts were robbing a woman over at that church," McDonald says, "and about five or six vets ran across the street with ball bats." They still have a video of it.

"We were cleaning up all the negative stuff that was going on around here," Sand says. "The cops would give us the thumbs-up."

There were the crack houses next door, right on Woodward, openly selling drugs. The vets eventually handled the issue themselves. "One of the guys, a marine, had a Caterpillar tractor; he was an excavator. He brought it in on a Sunday, and he bulldozed those joints out of here. And the cops go by and go, 'Thanks.'"

FOR YEARS THERE'S been an empty lot next door. Flowering trees shower the ground with red petals in the spring. The vets planted them a few years ago, with some grass and a flagpole, to mark the spot for a future memorial to Detroit veterans of all wars. It's a city-owned lot, but the vets say they had a long-standing agreement that allowed them to build a memorial there if they raised the funds.

But the city recently gave a company permission to park cars there, turning it into a mud pit after Lions and Tigers games down the street. Now their memorial project is in limbo as they get the runaround from the city on the future of the site.

Sand sees it as yet another fight to take something and make it better, as they did decades ago with the old building.

"It's just been a horrendous battle," he says. "It shouldn't be that way, but it's always been that way, from the day we got drafted till today and tomorrow when our kid comes home from Iraq and he's all jacked up. But we're gonna

Vietnam veteran Mike Sand on the site of his group's hoped-for memorial.

Chapter Nine holds a memorial service to commemorate the anniversary of the Fall of Saigon.

be there for him because we still wave our flag, we believe in this country, we give each other hope. It's just sad the city doesn't see that."

Inside, though, there's no mistaking whose place this is.

They've got a little bar in the building whose walls are blanketed with hundreds of old military snapshots, posters and news clippings gone brown. It's like an exhibit to be taken in slowly, because each little thing holds volumes of meaning to whoever put it there.

There's also a meeting hall that's ringed with large, framed photos of vets with stern or sorrowful expressions, snapshots from bittersweet parades, portraits of old friends long gone.

Over the years, this place has seen rallies and parades, hosted a mini-police precinct and Veterans Administration offices, reached out to the homeless veterans who still wander the neighborhood and brought in veterans coming home from recent wars. The people who started this, the ones who were initially reluctant to join, wound up staying forever and helping others who might have been lost without this place.

"Ninety percent of the people in the building here today are working, family oriented, just trying to give back," Sand says. "That's what we do."

Rites of Spring

An Outdated Ceremony for Girls Brings Lost Traditions to Life

THE DEBUTANTE STEPS into the spotlight, and a hush falls over the room.

She wears white satin gloves and white pearls and an airy, white billowing gown, and she shines as she stands under the light, at the edge of the ballroom and at the center of attention.

Her tuxedoed father has just escorted her down a marble staircase into the full gaze of the crowd assembled inside the lavish Crystal Ballroom of Detroit's Masonic Temple.

It's the Debutante Cotillion Ball, an old-fashioned southern ceremony, the unlikeliest of events, held in the ragged Cass Corridor, the unlikeliest of places.

As the pair slowly walks the long floor to the stage, the announcer reads off the debutante's credentials—her academic achievements, her volunteer activities, her athletic accomplishments, her goals. Each of the girls being honored here on this spring evening has a list just as long. To be selected for this night, they have to be achievers in academics and athletics and successes in their still-short lives.

Once on stage, facing the hundreds in the crowd, she descends slowly to the floor in a perfect curtsy that makes her long gown spread out gracefully at her feet.

And the crowd bursts into applause for her, for the night, for what this formal gesture represents.

"It goes back to our basic principles of returning social grace, poise, elegance to our lives and to our youth," says Renita Barge Clark, forty-two, the founder of the Cotillion Society, the group behind this evening's event. "It increases their self-esteem. It helps make them well-rounded individuals. Most of them have been exposed to some things, but here, we take it to another level."

A COTILLION, OR debutante ball, is the formal presentation of young ladies to polite society. Based on English tradition, it flourished in the American South after the Civil War. Back then it signified that a girl had reached maturity and was now ready to be courted for marriage by eligible bachelors of similarly high social status.

Nowadays, it serves mostly to sustain these quaint old customs, to pass on lost traditions and forgotten ways of behavior. For years, the Cotillion Club of Detroit hosted such balls, so nationally renowned that *Ebony* magazine devoted a four-page photo spread to it one year. Though the club began in 1946 as a social group for black businessmen and evolved over time into a political organization fighting for civil rights, every year it offered young black women the chance to participate in the southern traditions their migrating parents brought north with them.

But it folded in 1996. Clark, a local physician who'd gone through her own debutante ball as a teenager, didn't want to see these coming-of-age celebrations vanish from the area. A few years ago, she and a friend did some research, traveled the country to observe debutante balls and organized a nonprofit educational foundation, and last year they held their first cotillion.

For the high school juniors and seniors selected as debutantes, the road here is long and hard. "It's almost like a mini charm school," Clark says. There are the twice-weekly waltz practices that become weekly as the ball draws near. Months of etiquette lessons. Cultural outings like Brunch with Bach at the Detroit Institute of Arts and tickets to the Alvin Ailey American Dance Theater at the Detroit Opera House. Volunteer tutoring at the Sickle Cell Center in Detroit. Afternoon tea at the Townsend Hotel in Birmingham. Facets of culture that most girls nowadays don't get to experience.

"It really is sad," she says. "But hopefully as time goes on we as a whole society will feel the need to reinstate some of these traditions, because I believe there was true meaning and a purpose to them."

THE ESCORTS GATHER behind a set of French doors, just outside the ballroom. Their heads tilt toward a crack in the door as each waits to hear his name called.

Each debutante has her own escort, a teenage boy who is called to the ballroom floor to stand in the spotlight under the scrutiny of the audience. His achievements will be read aloud, he'll solemnly bow and he'll walk up to

The debutantes huddle backstage before the dance.

The escorts listen from behind the French doors, waiting to be called.

her father and formally ask for a dance with his daughter.

This is a lot to think about now, and the waiting escorts break the tension by clowning around, acting unconcerned, but every few minutes they fall back into expressions of mild nervousness as they listen in silence to hear their names.

That's the look worn by Blake West, sixteen, as he watches the escorts called before him and assesses what awaits him.

A University of Detroit Jesuit High School and Academy student, he will be majoring in engineering or business at Howard, Columbia, Morehouse or Georgetown, he declares with the assurance of someone whose future is already mapped out. The program for the evening spells out his record: track and field team, member of the Business Club at school, treasurer of Detroit Kappa League, volunteering with Toys for Tots, tutoring at night and so on—a kid with more responsibilities than most adults.

Like the others, he too went through the etiquette lessons, the dance practices, the instruction on table manners. "I think this is a very valuable experience, because when I grow up I may have to go to an event with the president, and those are some things to know," he says, already thinking big.

These are the kids who go to the good schools in town, come from good families, have high aspirations. Tonight is about celebrating them for simply doing good things with their lives.

"I'm very blessed," West says about his school, where most of his achievements have taken place. It's a nod to his awareness that fortunate circumstances make a difference too.

The announcer's voice echoes through the old hall. It's hard to discern her words from outside the ballroom. But one thing comes through clear. "Blake West." And with that, he goes through the door and steps into the spotlight.

FOUR DEBUTANTES PRECEDED her. Two will follow. But this is Lauren Roberts's time.

She attended last year's ball, watching the pageantry from the audience. It was so magical, so enchanting, that she applied to be one of those taking the long walk to the stage this year. She went through all the rigors—the application process, the etiquette lessons, the cultural tours, the self-improvement sessions—with six other girls just as eager to be part of this rarified world.

"I didn't know any of the girls before, but we were all really excited to be there, and all of us looking beautiful and growing closer together," the seventeen-year-old says. "We formed a bond for everything we accomplished."

Now, down those marble stairs she goes. Down to the edge of the room, where the spotlight pours onto her. Down the long dance floor to the stage. And down to the floor for the elegant curtsy, the exclamation point on all her efforts, the small but significant summation of the night and all that it means. "You get to stand up there while they read off all your accomplishments, and it made me feel really good

A debutante is formally presented by her father to the gathered crowd.

A debutante and her escort dance in the center of the ballroom.

Above, left: A debutante puts the finishing touches on an escort's tuxedo.
Above, right: He stands under the spotlight as his credentials are read aloud.

to be recognized like that," Roberts says. Of all the pageantry here—the formal etiquette, the beautiful gowns, the choreographed waltz, the precise movements—her favorite part is just being honored for her everyday accomplishments, those for a single, magnificent night and those for a life still ahead.

Clark watches from the shadows at the spectacle she's pulled off. And she beams.

"The hope is that we will make a positive impact on the city of Detroit and remind people that everything in Detroit is not bleak; that we do have shining jewels—these talented young ladies and men who will make a difference in society," Clark says.

Tomorrow the debutantes and escorts go back to normal life. But tonight, as they waltz beneath the hanging chandeliers of a magnificent old ballroom, they are celebrated for what they've done with those normal lives. Tonight they are stars.

"I kind of felt like it was my moment," Roberts says. "I felt beautiful."

Little Bar on the Prairie

An Iconic Restaurant Keeps Old Detroit Alive

MIKE HARNETT LEANS back against the hood of his car, arms folded, eyes alert. It's early afternoon, and everything is still and quiet in the fields around him.

His job is to watch over the cars of the customers at the Ivanhoe Café, better known as the Polish Yacht Club, a 101-year-old bar and restaurant on the corner of Frederick and Joseph Campau, where part of Poletown used to be.

"I'm like a scarecrow, more or less," the fifty-year-old says.

He's here as a reassuring presence to customers and a deterring one to criminals. "They say it's good to have somebody here when they come out the door," he explains.

Though he once thwarted someone trying to steal a catalytic converter off someone's vehicle, not much crime happens here because the location is so desolate. Most of the nearby residents are old folks, almost all the little stores that once were here are long gone and this neighborhood fixture doesn't have much of a neighborhood around it anymore.

"Did you have a good lunch?" Harnett says gently to a pair of older ladies as they make their way out the door. Wonderful, they say. He escorts them to their car.

Once they drive off it's quiet again but for the buzz of the bugs in the grass. And it stays quiet. A stray dog snorts through an alley. A breeze makes the tops of the wild trees sway. The sun beats down, and the shadows grow long as the day rolls on and not a soul comes by. It's as serene as a country road.

Yet Harnett stays on guard out here, over not just the cars but also a part of old Detroit, still around after all these years, hanging on like a flower in the weeds.

EVERYTHING ABOUT THE Polish Yacht Club is old-time. The name Ivanhoe refers to its original telephone exchange. The food is thick and rich, a throwback to an earlier style of dining. They serve big plates of perch and walleye and frog legs and kielbasa. Vegetables are scarce. Instead of a breadbasket, you get a stack of pickles. The atmosphere is casual, the prices are cheap and everything is made from scratch.

The décor inside reflects the look of restaurants a half century ago. The wall in the main dining room is covered with autographed portraits of local celebrities from years back, such as weatherman Sonny Eliot, sportscaster Ray Lane and Mayor Jerry Cavanagh.

Little candleholders with crosses on them dot the tables, as Polish as can be, as are the photos of Pope John Paul II that hang in one room. An antique piano sits near the kitchen. Nautical artifacts poke out high and low from the walls. Every room is small, reached through a narrow door, betraying the restaurant's origins as somebody's house. You're eating in the old living room one day, a child's former bedroom the next. It's home cooking in a real home.

The massive wood bar is the same one the locals drank at in 1909, under the same tin ceiling. Framed black-and-white pictures of neighbors who were regulars decades ago fill the rooms. Everything here announces that this place has a long history.

A man named Stanislaus Grendzinsk founded it in 1909. His daughter Agnes took over in the 1920s, adding a restaurant to what was just a bar. Her daughter's husband, Big John, ran it for forty-one years after that. He was a legend around here, the big personality behind the bar. Everyone still talks about him even though he died sixteen years ago. "My dad was awesome," says Patty Galen. Now, she and friend Tina Marks, both fifty-three, manage it; her mom, Lucille Sobczak, Big John's eighty-two-year-old widow, owns it. "The three girls," as Galen says. They're this era's familiar faces behind the bar.

Back in its heyday, the Ivanhoe anchored a block in what was a small town within a big city.

"There were a lot of places to park on the street because nobody had cars," Sobczak says of Poletown. "They took the streetcar or the bus. And there were stores all over. There weren't any real rich people, but there were cute little houses. They had a little bit of lawn and a porch, and people would sit on their porch. Detroit was a beautiful city."

For years the Ivanhoe was the neighborhood's place to be, where judges and politicians and businessmen let lunches stretch into the third or fourth drink.

Patty Galen (left) with Tina Marks inside the iconic Ivanhoe Café.

"In the '60s and '70s this place was like crazy-cuckoo," says Galen. "There would be a lineup outside." Back then, Big John had to buy three hundred pounds of fresh perch every week just to meet demand. Reservations were made not for the number of seats you needed but for how much fish you wanted.

But the neighbors started migrating out of the city, and the line outside dwindled. "Everybody that came here before the riots, they all lived close," Galen says. "Then they all started moving out to the suburbs, and it just got farther and farther to come to dinner."

This still bothers Sobczak, who, though she moved outside the city, never considered taking the restaurant with her. She grew up here, in the apartment upstairs.

"You know, there are some people that are scared to even come to Detroit," she says. "They're just scared of Detroit. But you know, bad things happen all over. A lot of places have problems." She still comes in every Friday to watch things over, say hi to old friends, be the link that connects then to now.

"People that we know have been coming here for fifty, sixty years," she says. "And they come in still, and it makes it real nice."

ITS COMMON NAME came from one of those old Polack-style jokes. A guy drinking at the bar in the early '60s was dodging his wife, and when she'd angrily call there looking to see if he was on a bender, he'd tell Big John to say he was over at the "Polish Yacht Club." This was a real hoot to his fellow drinkers, and the name stuck to the landlocked bar.

A few years later, though, the regulars decided to make it a real organization. They printed up silly membership cards, bought captain's sailing hats and jackets, held annual elections for a commodore and took a photo of the winner wearing the costume. A wall is now lined with dozens of these portraits from over the years, showing men whose closest connection to water was how much was used to cut their drinks. Members even once jokingly asked the Detroit City Council if a canal could be built from their doorstep to the river a few miles away so they wouldn't be landlocked anymore.

The club has monthly meetings and holds an annual gala dinner that raises money for such causes as juvenile diabetes and the nearby St. Hyacinth Church. It still has more than one hundred members, carrying on the kind of social traditions that have died off in so many other places around town.

Those traditions have helped Ivanhoe outlast everything around it. The nearby residents left and it stayed. Then the houses went away, leaving it standing alone on its block. Its bar lasted through Prohibition, its restaurant survived the Depression. All by keeping things the same even as everything around it changed.

As customers leave, nearly every one of them comes over to say goodbye to Galen or give her or her mom a hug.

"It's still a family business and we treat our customers like family," Galen says. "When you have something that works and something is good, why mess with it?"

The Fixer

How One Inner-City Man Battles to Earn an Honest Living

THEY'RE SWARMING AROUND him today—like they always do. And though he's waiting for customers, he's getting visits from everyone else.

It's a hot summer afternoon, and Gus Mills is seated on an overturned milk crate in a deserted parking lot. A hand-painted wood sign propped on the sidewalk announces his business: What it Dew Lawnmower Repair and Sales.

For two years now, every day but Sunday, the forty-seven-year-old spreads out his tools next to an abandoned dry cleaner on Gratiot near McNichols and sits in the deep shade of a wild tree sprouting from the side of a neighboring building.

He'll fix your broken lawnmower on the spot, usually within the hour. Repairs are a flat forty-five-dollar fee.

"It might be a couple of things wrong, but for forty-five dollars you're going home with it running, as opposed to when you take it to the other side of Eight Mile—they want thirty-five dollars just for you to walk into the building." He gets about a dozen customers a day.

He works from April to August, saving most of what he earns so he can attend community college the rest of the year. He's polite, hardworking, determined to project a professional image despite his rough surroundings.

But this makes him a target for hangers-on and hustlers. In this neighborhood, where a whole lot of people don't have jobs or much schooling or much of a future, a place where scrapping metal or selling drugs are common careers, a guy like Mills stands out for trying to do an honest day's work. He becomes a center of gravity, like a sun with lifeless planets orbiting him.

Mothers come up and demand that he teach their sons a job skill. Transients come looking for a couple hours' work. Men clutching bottles in bags pull up seats, flanking him in the shade, wasting his time and theirs, hoping for some scraps.

"I get the impression that everybody's watching me," Mills says, wearily. "Everybody comes up, they're like seagulls. And I'm tired of it. Go away— oh, man."

ON SOME DAYS, business gets so good that Mills could use some helpers. But few around this neighborhood are qualified. And the handful who do have skills don't have much of a work ethic. "I can't keep them. I give them a couple dollars and they're gone. Let a cat get twenty bucks, man, he's outta here. Then he'll come back, he's drunk, high and everything else."

Gus Mills in his parking lot, waiting for customers.

A pickup truck roars into the lot. "Speaking of the mechanics," Mills says, "here they come now."

The driver is young, maybe early twenties, and he's got the sly smile of a schemer. His passenger is older, dumber, possibly drunk and is missing all his top front teeth. He gets out of the truck and roams among the lawnmowers and the tools spread around Mills, while the driver distracts him with questions about a guy in the neighborhood, about the weather, about that old lawnmower sitting there. It's as though they can't decide whether to hustle him or work for him.

"You still got my number, right?" the driver asks. Mills shakes his head no. "I ain't seen you," he says. These two don't show up enough to be taken seriously as potential employees. "If I don't use a number within thirty days, it deletes." The driver's face becomes quizzical. A phone that deletes numbers on its own?

"But that's your new phone!" he protests. Mills just carries the ruse further. "I shouldn't even have said thirty days. If I don't see you within ten days, it deletes it," he says with a straight face.

They drive off, and Mills shakes his head.

"I call them Heckle and Jeckle," he says. "They're annoying. I mean, you see how they talk?"

HE GETS OTHER kinds of attention too. A beat-up pickup truck pulls up, driven by a middle-aged woman. She's a neighborhood junk collector, and she's got a thing for the lawnmower repair guy.

"Hey, you got a cellphone on you?" she asks, without saying hi. "My sister wants to ask you about something." He tells her no, he has no phone. Meanwhile, his phone pokes slightly out of his pocket.

The woman visits often, usually on some pretext to talk to him. Today it's supposedly a relative who has a question for Mills. The woman dials on her cellphone and hands it to him. "Tell her you the lawnmower man," she says. There's nobody on the other end, though. He gives her the phone back. She frowns, suddenly promises to return and drives off, as stacks of appliances and metal sheets rattle in the back of her junk truck.

"She wanted to go out," Mills explains, "and it was crazy. She would come and post up. I'd tell her I might close at four o'clock or five; man, she'd be here at three thirty and sit right over there. I'm waitin' on customers and I'd have to go tell her, 'Well, I'm gonna be here for another hour.' She'd leave, and I'd take off," he says, laughing.

In this neighborhood, a guy like Mills is a catch. He has a job, he has goals and he's respectful. For someone like the junk lady, he's gold. "But she's probably backed off a little," he says with relief.

MILLS SPENDS HIS days in this lot because he wants the building that sits here. As soon as the dry cleaner went out of business, he had his eye on it. It's got a big parking lot to the side and plenty of room for a waiting area and a workspace. Wait until it goes into foreclosure or tax lien, he figures, then snap it up and open his own small engine repair shop. None of that has happened yet, though.

He's not the only one eyeing that building. Scrappers noticed it too.

"Scavengers, man, they just demolished it," he says. "I've called the police on some guys going in there. And I have had some altercations. They wanted to be belligerent to me— 'Mind your own business' and blah blah. I have to tell them, 'You guys don't scare me.'" But the electrical system is already gone. So's the plumbing. The building becomes more worthless by the day.

A thin, sweaty little man rides up on a bicycle and begins tinkering with his bike, using Mills's tools without asking. Mills knows him; the man volunteers to do cleanup for him sometimes. It's either ironic or nervy. "He's the same joker—I wanted this building, and he stripped it," Mills says. In this rough area, a dead building is up for grabs. So is everything else.

"Oh, my goodness," he says. "You name it, brother; you'll see it through here. This is the most action that any one man should be able to see unless he's going to Vietnam or somewhere."

Last year he watched a man running past on Gratiot get shot in the back and collapse in the middle of the road in front of him. Just the other day he saw a band of kids chasing someone, shooting wildly. "The newer dudes, the younger kids nowadays, man, they can be bananas coming through here, running through here. Just as long as they stay away from me."

Compared to that, a scrapper is benign. And this one sits right next to the man whose dream he's dismantling, pipe by pipe.

A FEW DAYS pass, and Mills sits in his spot under the high sunshine, but no customers pull into the lot. The pests are intimidating to people, and today the pests are swarming.

There's little Mills can do about them. This abandoned lot isn't his. It's everyone's by default. He could move to another spot, but this is the neighborhood where he grew up, and this is where he wants to be. And he wants to keep watch on that building.

"It's crazy. The little peace that I want I just can't get to," he says, defeat in his voice. "I'm just tired."

As the hot day wears on, four raggedy guys amble up and sit behind him, talking among themselves, while Mills just sits silently with his head in his hands and his eyes looking down.

Stayin' Alive

An Old Tradition Struggles to Hang On
in a Detroit Neighborhood

LOUIE PACINI'S BUSINESS is as fragile as the brittle creations he makes.

He's a craftsman whose plaster statues have been crowded out of the marketplace by cheap imitations from China. His health is faltering, tormented by persistent cancer. His customers have moved away, taking with them their patronage. And his employees were let go, one by one, as people stopped buying the delicate little things he makes.

"Right now, it's just down to me," he says. He owns Sam Pacini Statues on Van Dyke, just south of Eight Mile. "The only reason I survive is I'm by myself; the building is paid for; I got no overhead, but even now it's a struggle to even stay in business."

His species is endangered—a Michigan manufacturer engaged in an obscure art inside a little shop in a Detroit neighborhood. "You can drive right by and you don't even know we're here," he says.

But he still comes to work every day, locks the door behind him and heads back to his workshop, where he molds wet plaster into vases, planters, statues and figurines, using a technique that goes back centuries.

His finished creations line long aisles of shelves in his shop, streaming from one end of the store to the other by the hundreds. Almost all of them are soft, white and delicate, giving them a ghostly look in the dim light. Unfinished simple frogs and pigs share shelf space with traditional statues of Catholic saints whose detailed faces are etched with agonized or beatific expressions.

In the old days, he had to hustle to compete with others like him who carried on this tradition. Now there are fewer craftsmen and fewer customers.

"There's really nobody in the state doing this now, but back when we took over there were shops all over the place," he says. "We're the only ones in Michigan doing this now."

PACINI'S FAMILY CAME to Detroit by way of Chicago from Lucca, Italy, a little town famous for its plaster figurines. There's even a museum there dedicated to the long history of its craftsmen.

"Everybody there pretty much was in this type of business, the statue business," Pacini says. His voice still hints at the accent he's left with from his first eight years in Italy. "My mom went back there a few years ago and said there's still shops putting the stuff outside to dry, letting it air dry."

The town craftsmen began emigrating a couple hundred years ago; some eventually wound up in the American Midwest, a few made their way to Detroit and one family brought the tradition to the little shop on Van Dyke.

The store was named after his uncle. And his dad. Amazingly, they had the same first and last names, despite being unrelated, at least until one Sam Pacini married into a family that happened to have another Sam Pacini. The uncle who founded the store was Louie's mother's brother.

"Coincidence," he says. "Pacini is, in our part of the town we came from, like Johnson or Smith is here."

Sam Pacini the uncle died in 1978 and left the business to Sam Pacini the father. No name change was necessary.

Pacini uses techniques passed through generations of his family in Italy.

Opposite: The unpainted plaster pieces have a ghostly look in the dim light.

"At the time, we were living in Chicago," Pacini says. "My dad actually did this type of work in Chicago, and when my uncle passed away he wasn't married or anything, so we pretty much inherited the business, and that's when we moved here."

The family, like most in Lucca, had its own way of making plaster. "Our technique, nobody does it the way we do it," he says. "I learned everything about it from my dad. I learned how to make little stuff, then from there I graduated to the bigger pieces, and then I was eventually able to do everything."

Pacini's dad died not long after moving to Detroit, leaving his son in charge. His mom would help out sometimes, but she was getting older and soon stopped coming around. It became his shop.

Back then, three decades ago, business was booming. "We were doing pretty good with it for a little place like this," he says. On some days he'd have eight employees working at once in the back. He would hire the kids from the shop's crime-ridden neighborhood and teach them the craft.

"I hired all the degenerates," he says, half-joking. "People don't realize, even a little place like us, I hired people that nobody else was going to hire. And you need that, especially in the city. And we've lost so many of the small businesses that would do that."

There were benefits to hiring locally—when crime skyrocketed in the area and break-ins started happening at the shop, his employees would use their street connections to find out who did it and send a message, verbal or otherwise, that the store was off limits.

"The guys who used to work for me were probably some of the worst guys in the neighborhood, so actually they kind of watched out for me," he says.

Despite their rough lifestyle, the kids would always show up for work on time, Pacini notes. One stands out in his mind.

"One time he came in, he got shot in the hand; he had blood coming out the hand a little bit and he was still coming to work. Another time he got stabbed in the back and he didn't even tell us. And he was working, and I could tell he was in pain. He had a cut this big," he says, holding his hands about a foot apart. "Somebody sliced him because he sold some crackhead some soap and they cut him."

But then the economy soured, cheap statues from places like China poured in, business dried up and employees had to be let go. Pacini got thyroid cancer and closed the shop while he sought treatment, and when he came back, his customers had moved on.

Louie Pacini with a century-old church statue of St. Anthony that he restored.

"The health issue set me back a little bit, but what can you do? That stuff happens. But everything goes in cycles. That's why I figure if we can stick this out there's always something that comes along." He still always says "we" out of habit when speaking of the shop, even though he's the only one here now.

The Pacini workshop has been coated in plaster over the years, one drop at a time.

THE WALLS OF the workshop are splattered with plaster. Thick drops of it cake the wood benches where the finished statues are left to dry. Years of work have left their mark in the shop, one drop at a time, one day at a time. The workshop is almost like an artwork in itself.

Making a statue takes time. Pacini starts by mixing water with fine white plaster powder. The mixture is poured into a latex-coated mold, then poured back out, leaving a paper-thin coating. Once that dries, he does it again. And again. He repeats the process until there's a quarter-inch-thick layer inside, brittle and thin but strong. The statues are hollow, and this is how they are made, from the outside in.

Finally, the mold is pulled away and the plaster piece is left to dry.

These days he sells a handful at a time, mostly to hobbyists or gift shops that keep a few of the figurines in stock. Some teachers buy them for the kids in their classes to paint. A brush and some paints cost only a few dollars. The kids love them, he says. It's an easy way for them to create something artistic.

When he became ill a few years back, he put a For Sale sign in the front window. Predictably, on a street where empty buildings have gone unused for decades, there have been no inquiries. "I'm going to take it down," he says. "Ain't nothing going to happen."

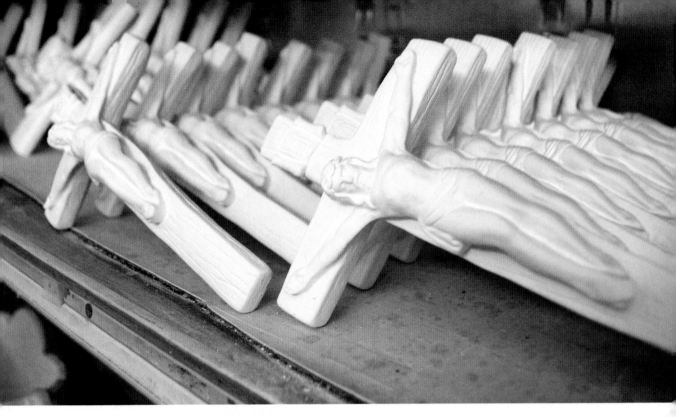

Rows of pale crucifixes line a long shelf.

His craft survived a trip across the ocean, the deaths of two owners, a bad economy, a brutal illness, cheap imitations of his work and changing decorative tastes. Yet it stays alive because he wills it to, because he's never done anything else, but mostly because he still loves making those little statues. This craft is his life.

"I'm gonna be forty-nine years old, so it's like, 'What am I gonna do now?'" he wonders in those moments when he thinks of giving up and closing for good. "This is what I know. This is *all* I know."

In So Many Words

An East Side Old-Timer Who Never Runs Out of Ideas

LEROI HASKINS IS a man of many words.

When he speaks, they come out in elaborate sentences that spin out into tangents and then loop back around again. So many of them swirl in his head that they've spilled out over the years into dozens of essays and books.

"I got four or five books coming up in the next year," the eighty-eight-year-old says cheerfully. He's a gentle old man with a baroque writing style and a merry laugh. His whole face takes part in his smile. "I am always writing a book inside of me. I can never finish all the books I want to write."

The eccentric longtime activist heads the Community Information and Advisory Council, which he founded with several other parents in 1968 to fight the elimination of a few grade levels from their east side neighborhood school.

Their efforts didn't work, but Haskins has kept the CIA alive to this day, giving him a platform from which to protest or organize neighbors for a cause.

He sends extravagant letters to presidents and senators. He posts short essays on a website about wide-ranging topics, including the lottery, juvenile delinquents and advice on how to pay down credit card debt, which is addressed to a fictional everywoman he calls "Martha Doe." He even ran for mayor of Detroit in 1993 and got a few dozen votes.

And whenever an issue gets him riled up, he writes a book about it. The stories of police brutality told to him by a cop became a book. The poor conditions he found as an investigator in a youth home became a book. Even the trouble he had with his Veterans Administration mortgage after a missed payment became a book. He literally dreamed an entire book once, about the John F. Kennedy assassination. There are several others, and

LeRoi Haskins's house is a museum of carefully preserved old styles.

many more that have yet to make the transition from thoughts in his head to words on a page.

"The weird thing is, he does not read. He has never been a reader," says Carolyn Ramsay, sixty-seven, an adjunct ESL instructor at the University of Detroit Mercy and Henry Ford Community College. She's a longtime friend who helps transcribe the books he dictates aloud in his signature prose. "He just has his totally own style. They're pretty long, complicated sentences. I don't have to make very many grammar corrections, but stylistically it's like, oh my God."

For example, the self-penned back cover of one of his books reads, "What should be of special interest to you, the reader, is that any and all of the materials of this story represent a self-imposed recreation by the author of a series of related revelations—revelations that once assembled produced this complete and rather unique, as well as profound explanation." He speaks like this too.

Of all his causes, the one that underlies everything he says and does is his dream of a colorblind society, one where, he says, race isn't a defining characteristic. "I've never lived in a home in my eighty-eight years of life where the terms 'black' and 'white' were accepted. Never," he says. "You get to the point you don't use it. It's not a part of you. It doesn't come up."

It came up a lot, though, when he was growing up.

His earliest memory is of an angry crowd marching past his family's house in Kentucky. "There was a lynching mob coming down the street, going to lynch somebody in Owensboro," he says. "It was impressed on my brain."

He was drafted into the army in World War II and sent to England, where he served as a mapmaker. The white soldiers would tell the townspeople that Haskins and his fellow black soldiers had tails. "They believed it actually," Haskins says. "They'd never seen a black person."

A sympathetic white commanding officer looked out for him and shielded him to a degree. "I'll never forget him," he says. "He loved me." But the officer was transferred midway through the war. "He said, 'Mr. Haskins, they're gonna give you all kind of problems.' I said, 'I know it.' He said, 'I can take you with me,' and I said, 'I can't leave my men. These men depend on me. They'll do anything I ask them to do.' And I stayed. And I caught hell."

His replacement didn't like blacks and didn't like Haskins. "He was from Texas. He thought I was the most proud black person on planet Earth. He wanted to destroy me. And he did a pretty good job." The officer hounded him, baited him, eventually getting him demoted.

Once home, at a factory job, he got in trouble for talking to a white girl. "I was told, 'I understand you were giving time in the aisleway to a particular Caucasian woman,'" he remembers. "I took a stand then. At that particular moment I decided that I had to go out there and inform the community of what is our greatest problem, the greatest problem is trying to live in a world of black and white people. You can't do it."

Yet despite everything, he's held firm to an old-fashioned kind of American idealism. He quotes Abraham Lincoln and the Constitution the way some people quote the Bible. His website features an a cappella audio file of him singing "America the Beautiful" slowly and reverently, like it's a spiritual hymn. His stone front porch steps are painted red, white and blue. An American flag flies

The always interesting LeRoi Haskins at his piano.

high on a pole in his backyard. It's quaint and charming and heart touching, seeing this earnest little elderly fellow still strong in his beliefs despite a life that sometimes argued against them.

He married twice, had seven children, worked different jobs, volunteered, led a men's choir and headed a church-sponsored recreational program for kids that included Sonny Banks, the first boxer to knock down Cassius Clay (as he was then known) in a fight, he proudly notes.

And then the books started coming forth, about a dozen so far, he thinks. They aren't really selling right now, he says, but he hopes things will improve with his website, which features pitches in his formal yet freewheeling style: "Each book will allow the reader to have a more in-depth appreciation and knowledge of the various factors that shape the world in which we live, its people, and the events that follow. While some books may be intended only for enjoyment, with others a greater reward may be anticipated." His beliefs contain a hint of conspiracy and a dose of populism, always expressed politely.

His eyesight has grown very poor, bad enough that he can't see his way around his house, bad enough not to notice that some kid recently tore his new tree down out front, until a neighbor told him. Ramsay, his closest friend, escorts him by arm from room to room, or else he feels his way around as he shuffles forward, achingly slow.

He lives alone in a house as quirky as his prose. The living room is pink. A vintage starburst clock sits above a fireplace. The main couch is covered in plastic. Neatly printed aphorisms he penned are framed and hung on the walls. Several books he's written are displayed on a table. The dust cover of one notes of its oddball author: "Mr. Haskins endeavors to be an outstanding humanitarian. His hobbies are writing, piano composition, sports and group conversation."

And still he writes, dictating long works to the ever-patient Ramsay, often under the rubric of his CIA, which more often than not consists pretty much just of him. But when he gets going on something, really gets talking, it's a linguistic adventure.

"I'm saying there is a life beyond this life, I'm not getting into that at the stage of what I'm doing as far as what's going to be done in CIA Council," he begins. "If we are going to do something, you and I in our lives, we have to anticipate there is another world, there's something beyond life, beyond our lives, it's in that context that I'm trying to rush now, or get to a point to show the only way out is for that big ball of fire up there to take over..." Many sentences later, it's still not clear what he's trying to say, but it's fascinating just to follow along.

Ramsay sits nearby, bemused. "I guess that's why I stick around," she says. "It's always interesting.

Petal Pushers

An Old-Fashioned Florist Counts the Days Until the End

ONCE VALENTINE'S DAY passed, things got slow again at the flower shop.

Life here is marked by flower-driven holidays, and between those busy dates, it gets real quiet. There's no radio on, not much traffic is heard passing down the street and people don't often walk past the front windows anymore.

Roy Szymanski has come to rationalize away the lulls. "You can't be busy every day," the sixty-six-year-old says. He has worked at St. Hedwig Flower and Gift Shop in southwest Detroit for more than forty years. "You never know what comes in between—a funeral happens or somebody you know passes away, then naturally you're going to get to work on that day."

This time, the big event is the installation of officers at the local Knights of Columbus hall, a celebration that calls for floral arrangements. "There's a centerpiece and table pieces and corsages for the ladies," Roy notes enthusiastically. He and owner Gus Turza, seventy-five, will be putting them together on Sunday. It's normally their day off, but at a little shop like this in the city, you never turn down business nowadays.

St. Hedwig's on Junction takes its name from the cross street it's on, which takes its name from the old Polish church that towers next door. Flowers have been sold from this building for more than eighty years. The motto here is "Flowers Are Always Nice."

It's a small, charming place. The air is saturated with the scent of the rose blooms that poke out of buckets in the cooler. Floating balloons and stuffed bears light up the store with bright reds and yellows, and the pink walls lend the room a gentle air. An ancient cash register sits unused on the counter, slathered in so much pink paint it won't open.

Two walls show cabinets with sliding glass doors that hold hundreds of quaint little statues, mugs and trinkets. And in the middle of the store, a small stand holds a few dozen vintage greeting cards.

All the extras have been here to carry them through the lean stretches between the busy holidays, which aren't really that busy anymore.

"We sell odds and ends," Szymanski says, looking over the miscellany. "You gotta carry a little bit of everything. Not a lot, but enough to keep going."

But it won't be going for much longer. "It's been a long time," Turza says with a sigh. He wants to retire. And once he closes the doors, they'll be closed for good.

ST. HEDWIG'S IS an unusual place. A chain card store like Hallmark wouldn't have thirty-year-old greeting cards with dated imagery selling for a mere dime apiece. A suburban gift shop wouldn't stock dainty figurines appreciated these days mostly by elderly ladies. Most florists wouldn't have a puppy wandering freely in the back, chewing stray flower stems.

But they've remained frozen in time by remaining hidden, like so many other little businesses tucked away in far-flung parts of the city, shielded from competition and the pressures of modernity. "It's old-fashioned, so we keep it old-fashioned," Szymanski says. "We keep it old-fashioned because people are used to it."

They rely for their traffic mostly on longtime loyal customers, people living nearby who don't want to drive to the suburbs for flowers and people who moved away but still come back for nostalgic reasons. "I've had people call and say, 'You did my mother's wedding. Can you do mine?'" Szymanski says.

Their stock hasn't changed in years. Neither has what they charge. "They're the same price they've always been," says Turza. "A lot of the prices have been there for years." Only the cost of the flowers has kept pace with the market.

The figurines remain cheap because there's not much demand for them. "The younger people don't really buy them," Szymanski says. "I'm not crazy for the figurines either. They're here just because they've always been here."

Over the years, business has gradually dried up. There are fewer people living nearby than when it opened, so their natural customer base is smaller. The shop isn't on a commercial strip, so few shoppers come to the area. Mostly though, he says, people nowadays get their cards at chain drugstores, and flowers can be bought at the grocery stores. The special things little shops like these sell aren't that special anymore.

Florists Roy Szymanski (left) and Gus Turza inside their old-fashioned flower shop.

"Everybody's got them," Szymanski complains. "You can go to Meijer, Kroger, they all carry flowers. You can go to any grocery store and get greeting cards. ACO Hardware even has them. Years ago you never had that. They're taking the business away from everybody that's small. Big business today is trying to take over everything."

THE TWO MEN met forty-five years ago in a little bar in Ohio. They got to talking and found out that Turza's grandmother had lived in the flat below the Szymanskis on Detroit's east side when both men were kids. "It's a small world," Szymanski says.

Turza found the little flower shop for sale in the late '60s and invited Szymanski to join him here. The woman selling it had owned it since the Depression, until her husband died and left her alone with their store and his gambling debts. She sold one to pay off the other. "She was like, 'What am I gonna do without my husband?' She just wanted to get rid of everything," Szymanski says. "She wasn't thinking right." Turza bought it, and the woman moved into an apartment upstairs, where she stayed for thirty more years, helping out now and then in the shop she used to own.

Four decades later, the two men want to retire and now face what so many longtime business owners in the city deal with—the truth that everything they've worked for is ending. There's nobody to pass the shop on to, because a place like this, in a city like this, can't make enough money to survive.

"This was the worst Christmas we've ever had," Szymanski says, thinking back to last year. Poinsettias used to carry the season. "We had this one lady that ordered for a church, she'd order fifteen plants or twenty plants for church at ten dollars a crack. She couldn't afford them this year. She called and said she was sorry. She's ninety-something years old and said, 'I just can't do it no more.'" She was so loyal that, instead of simply not showing up anymore, she felt she had to call and explain. At these old-time neighborhood stores, when a customer breaks his or her buying routine, it's noticed. Lately, she's not the only one making that phone call to them.

Across the street, a pile of cinders and charred wood that used to be another building housing small businesses rots in the sun. Szymanski says he sat with neighbors at the picnic table under the tree next to the store and watched it burn down one evening last year.

"There was a cleaners across the street, there was a doctor, a dentist, all this stuff, and now they're all gone. They moved out, stores got empty, then they started burning them down. And that's like anywhere in Detroit."

That's how old stores go away here, he says. Szymanski figures the same will happen when he and Turza retire. Sometimes, the ending for a place like his isn't a happy one.

"We'll close it down and they'll probably burn it down," he says, resigned. "In this neighborhood, who knows? Or it'll be an empty building. Just another one to join all the others that are around."

The Real Deal

How One Man Turned Himself into Santa

IT TURNS OUT that there really is a Santa Claus.

Did you know, though, that he lives not at the North Pole but in the Nortown neighborhood on the city's east side? Not only that, his sled isn't pulled by reindeer power but rather by horsepower and Detroit steel. And contrary to what the movies and the Christmas cards show, Santa is black.

"The youngsters make comments about that," says Santa, who during the rest of the year hides his true identity under the name Myron Benford. "You know that song by James Brown, 'Santa Claus Go Straight to the Ghetto'? They say, 'Finally! Now we see a brother Santa!' But I stay away from the color scene and just say, 'Well, now you've seen Santa in living color.'"

The sixty-six-year-old Benford, a retired Wayne County Road Commission employee, has for forty-two years brought Santa alive for Detroiters. It began when he got the familiar red-and-white, soft-and-fuzzy costume, which he'd wear while volunteering during the holidays. First it was with the Goodfellows, who'd give him the names and addresses of needy children; then later, he did it on his own at hospitals, schools, housing projects and youth homes, where he'd give less-fortunate kids a chance to talk to the season's icon in the flesh.

The children would get so excited by his visits that he was moved to buy toys at year-end clearance sales with his own money and save them until the next Christmas so he could hand them out when he made his rounds, to really fulfill the role.

Becoming Santa became an obsession. He pored over the songs and fairy tales, studied all the Christmas movies, even learned a few words of a few

Santa Benford with his reindeer-led Dodge Caravan sleigh.

languages so he could talk to even more kids, just like the Santa in the movie *Miracle on 34th Street*.

A few years back he took a 1992 Dodge Caravan, shaved off the roof, sheathed the car in red-painted cardboard and turned it into a big sleigh, led by two large Fiberglas reindeer affixed to the front. The car rides low, so when a few inches of snow lie on the ground, it almost looks like the sleigh is floating smoothly along as the reindeer pull it forward. The sight of it stuns people.

"I bring it as a package," he says. "It blows you away, it just does. When you see me, I'm the real deal. I mean, I make a point of it."

Imagine the things going through the mind of a little kid growing up in some housing project in Detroit when this strange, fantastic sled glides up, strung around its edges with garlands of colored tree lights, led forward by two big reindeer, with Santa Claus riding high in the middle. As if that's not enough, he steps out, larger than life, and starts handing out gift-wrapped presents to kids whose names he somehow knows.

Just like the Christmas stories say he does.

"It's just the idea of seeing the fantasy of that sled pull up in front of your house and you get out, give 'em a bag of toys and disappear. It really builds up their feelings. It's just miraculous."

WORD SPREAD ABOUT this gentle, self-appointed Santa, and he soon found himself in demand around town. Community groups asked him to visit holiday functions so kids could tell him what they wanted for Christmas. Cities brought him in for story time at their rec centers.

For years he's held court at Midtown's Noel Night at the Detroit Historical Museum. There, after you wind past the Lionel trains and walk along the cobblestone streets in the basement, you'll find Santa, sitting like royalty in a plush red chair with Mrs. Claus as gleeful kids and curious adults wait for their annual meeting with the man of the hour. Some of the grown-ups even sit on his lap.

"Especially the ones that are looking for a husband," he says, laughing. "They would come and tell me, 'I'm looking for a husband.' And the one lady a

Santa interacting with his fan base at a community center children's event.

- 113 -

Bedford finds that even the adults are drawn to Detroit's own Santa.

couple years ago...I said, 'I sent you one but you didn't like him because he wasn't tall enough.' And she says, 'How did you know that, Santa?'"

He's got lots of intuitive phrases he uses, especially with the kids, things he's learned after years of hearing people's fondest wishes. "You pick up the vibe of people," he says. "It's not a hard thing to do, and they help you if you just listen to them." It gives him the air of someone who knows exactly how you've been behaving all year.

Over the years, a few people have chipped in to help him buy his presents. Mechanics fix his sleigh-on-wheels for free. CVS and McDonald's give him donations and gift cards. And local organizations like Volunteers of America provide him a list of needy people who could use a cheerful visit from this man who really has become Santa Claus.

"I play it even when I'm not into it," he says. "When people introduce me during the rest of the year, they'll say, 'This is Santa.' They know what I do."

ALL HIS EFFORTS—STUDYING the Santa lore, gathering the gifts, upgrading the sleigh—come down to a single day of the year.

On Christmas Eve, Benford rises before the sun does, fills his bag with toys and makes his rounds. The sleigh ride begins at Jefferson Avenue, passes through the ghost town streets of Delray, follows the winding river to stops in Wyandotte and Ecorse, then turns back north and rides as far west as Southfield before slowly making its way back to the east side.

And all along the way he'll hand out hundreds of presents to hundreds of children, who in their wildest dreams never expected something like this. In the poorer neighborhoods, he'll give out hats and scarves and gloves, too, even such household items as smoke detectors and first aid kits.

"I want to make my kids well all year long," he says. "So that's how subliminally I'll reach the people I deal with out here, so they know I'm concerned about them all the time, not just at Christmas."

People who happen to be standing outside as the sleigh passes by stare with jaws dropped. Cars actually come to a stop on the main roads as people pull over to stare at this otherworldly vehicle going by. Some get out and run over to get a picture.

"I don't believe it," one man says, rushing over to the parked sleigh with his cellphone camera. "This is cold-blooded!" It was meant as high praise.

Benford loves the attention, lives to give out presents, doesn't break character and will always stop so someone can take a photo with him or the sleigh. But he seems happiest those times he's able to foster people's simple belief that there really is someone who goes around being nice and giving things to everyone just because it's Christmas.

"I've had people tell me their kids didn't believe in Santa Claus until they saw me, and now they do," he says, proudly, speaking through the curls of his thick, pull-on beard. "It's just great, man."

Magic Bus

Enlivening Lives One Book Stop at a Time

SHE WAS WAITING for him at the window.

For part of the morning, Marion Jenkins sat at a table, eating a bowl of Shredded Wheat in her fourth-floor apartment at McCauley Commons, a housing complex for seniors. The TV blared daytime shows in the background.

Jenkins, eighty-one years old and barely five feet tall, had seen the Detroit Public Library's bookmobile pull up outside and watched as Aaron Jacobsen, its forty-one-year-old librarian, stepped out with bags of books and walked into her building's lobby. She had fixed up her hair that morning, she says, in anticipation of his monthly visit.

He was due here at exactly eleven, but the time came and passed with no knock on the door. She grew dismayed and wondered, did he forget about me?

"I got a chance to get real sharp and he's not coming," she says. "He'd be up here by now."

But as doubt grows and minutes pass, a knock finally comes, and standing in the doorway is the guest of honor, holding two heavy-hanging department store bags full of books, dozens of them, courtesy of the Library on Wheels, the DPL's mobile unit that for years has been known around town simply as the bookmobile.

She's thrilled about the books, but she's happy just for his visit really, because Jacobsen is one of her few contacts nowadays.

"He's a doll," she says of him. "He's one of my boyfriends right here, but he doesn't know it."

Jenkins falls into that category loosely referred to as shut-ins, people who for whatever reason almost never leave their home to go into the world. The world has to come to them.

"It's a absolutely wonderful service for the seniors that can't get out," says Pam Duncan, the administrative manager at McCauley Commons. "A lot of them don't have transportation and are just physically unable to get out, and some of them don't have family to take them."

This is the first of many visits to shut-ins that the bookmobile has this morning. A librarian and a driver make rounds like this around town five days a week, two weeks out of every month, bringing within these books a glimpse of people and places these people would never otherwise see.

"It's kind of their way to get out, reading all these different things," says Ryan Boyd, the twenty-nine-year-old bookmobile driver. "You run into people, you can just kind of tell they don't get out at all, and we are their only contact."

This program was known in blunter days as Service to Shut-ins and Retirees before undergoing several name changes. But the mission remains the same. In a city where half the population can't read, they'll bring the written word to just about anyone who wants it. Along their routes, every stop they make is a glimpse into someone's private, reclusive world, one that few from the outside see.

Except for the guys from the bookmobile, who are not only welcomed into these homes but also find themselves regarded as more than just deliverymen. They're enlisted as helpers, as company, as substitutes for family members who've died or who don't bother coming by anymore.

"They've learned to trust you," says Carolyn McCormick, sixty-seven, the coordinator of specialized services in charge of the bookmobile. "You're their family."

THE DPL HAS operated its bookmobile since 1940. The program is based at the Douglass Branch for Specialized Services on Grand River near Trumbull, which also houses several other programs, like the Library for the Blind and Physically Handicapped.

Two bookmobiles make the rounds. Each one, a newer-model mini-bus with shelves instead of seats, can hold thousands of books.

One is full of children's material and makes stops at public schools in Detroit where the libraries have been closed or aren't staffed by a librarian anymore, rendering them closed anyway.

Aaron Jacobsen (left), with his bags full of books, and driver Ryan Boyd inside the bookmobile.

The other is stocked with genres such as mystery, romance, biography and modern novels. It visits far-flung homes, densely packed senior apartment complexes and riverfront retirement communities, serving adults who can't make their way to a library on their own. New patrons come by word of mouth or by postings on bulletin boards in recreation centers and retirement homes.

Sometimes the bus pulls up and people will come to browse inside the climate-controlled vehicle. If someone requests a title they don't have that day, the librarian will special order it and bring it next time.

The job has become more challenging, though. Layoffs in the past year cut the number of bookmobile drivers down from four to one. And mechanical issues with the bus intended for schools means they're down to one bookmobile. Every week, one set of books has to be hauled off it and replaced by another set.

On every route the bookmobile is staffed by two employees—Boyd, now the lone driver, and a librarian whose job it is to drag heavy bags of books up flights of stairs and down long hallways. Today, it's Jacobsen's shift.

Boyd, who comes from Ohio and who heard of the job opening from his father-in-law, himself a DPL employee, has been here a year and a half. Jacobsen, who moved to Detroit from Nevada to attend Wayne State University, has worked here seven years. Both men, warm and friendly with their customers, love the work and speak with real affection for those they visit.

"What I love about this is, you meet the seniors and they're good souls—the smile in their eyes, the smile on their faces," Jacobsen says. "I'm serious about what I do, but I want them to enjoy the experience, no matter how brief. I want them to come away positive. I like to get the person to smile. I'll do something silly, I don't care how old you are."

NEXT STOP IS a house on a curved east side street where half the homes are boarded up and the other half look like they soon could be.

It might be the strangest stop of the day. Jacobsen climbs creaky wood stairs to the second floor of an old Tudor duplex and enters another isolated world. The walls of the sparsely furnished living room and dining room are covered in spray-painted gang tags. One reads "Grand mafia kings bitch." Another claims this house for the Green Boyz. Holes dot the walls between the scrawlings. And in this setting live two frail women.

"We're trying to get it pulled together, remodel it, because it was damaged," says Gail Jackson, fifty-five, the home's new owner. It was a foreclosure they got on the cheap. The place had been empty and ransacked, tagged and torn up. Now they were trying to reclaim it as a home. "We just haven't gotten it together yet. It takes time," she says, softly.

She's tethered to an oxygen tank whose hose ropes around her head to feed air into her nose. Though she walks, she's too sick to get out anymore since she developed chronic obstructive pulmonary disease a few years ago. "I don't smoke," she explains. "It was environmental."

Jackson used the bookmobile for years, back before she got sick, back when she lived in a nice riverfront apartment, when its visit was a luxury, not a necessity. Now she relies on it because she can't get out anymore.

"It's exciting, you know, to get these books when they come once a month," she says. "We love the bookmobile. We love the library. We're avid readers." Along the wall, two shopping bags full of already-read books affirm her point.

She lives here with her mother, Blanche Taylor, seventy-eight, who sits at a small foldout table with a large, plastic machine in front of her and a wooden cane across her lap. She went blind two years ago and she too doesn't leave the house much anymore.

Now she devours books using a specialized, old-fashioned tape player loaned to patrons like her, using cartridges containing long volumes that fill the air with hours of prose at a time.

"Everybody needs to know about the bookmobile," she says. "I'm fortunate to get the audio books from the library, which I didn't know existed, but which has been great for me because I love to read, and I haven't been able to since I can't see. It's just been a blessing."

Jacobsen, now running behind on the route because everyone wants to talk with him a while, says a polite goodbye, turns and leaves behind him two dedicated readers in a battered house full of words—in books, on tape and all over the walls.

IT'S HARD FOR them not to get attached to the people they visit. But when all your customers on these runs are elderly, those you befriend may not be around for long.

"It's gotten me a couple of times," Jacobsen says. "It really has. You're not supposed to get possessive, but they're such good people and they can pass away in the night, and you're just like, wow. It's just all shock. But this is part of the reality of the program, dealing with seniors."

Sometimes they get the call from a family member, canceling the service because the patron has passed away. Other times they find this out firsthand.

McCormick, who's been with the library on and off for twenty-six years, has heard from employees who have walked in and found someone near death on the couch, or collapsed on the floor, or lying still in their beds.

The ones who come to the door on their own often press a librarian into service, asking them to do things like grab something off a high shelf, or mail a letter for them, or otherwise just keep them company because it's the only human contact they'll have for a long time.

"We're somebody that sees them, and we're somebody they know they can depend on once something is wrong," McCormick says. She points out that many grow to trust the bookmobile librarians so much they leave the door open for them to come in, especially if they're bedridden. But the librarians never know what they might find once they walk inside.

"It's not always good," McCormick says.

THE CITY'S LIBRARY system has been in the news a lot lately—budget woes, spending controversies, layoffs and threatened branch closings. Just about everyone on this route has heard these stories and is rattled and asks about it.

"They worry about us," McCormick says. "They're like, 'Are you sure you're going to be OK? How is this going to affect you?' And they want to give you their little ten and fifteen dollars, because they want to do everything they can to keep the service and keep the libraries open. Detroiters have always liked their libraries."

She says despite the city's ongoing budget problems, the bookmobile is safe. In fact, her branch won the National Library Service Award last month, and she and the staff have been invited to Washington, D.C., to be honored.

"With all the mess that has been going on, we were really glad to hear that we were doing something good here at Detroit Public Library," she says.

"NOW I'M GONNA fuss with you, Aaron. Where's your jacket?"

Julie Milner, an eighty-year-old living on the sixth floor of the River Towers senior apartments along the Detroit River, is hounding Jacobsen because it's a windy day outside and she thinks he'll catch a chill. If Jenkins in McCauley Commons thinks of him as her boyfriend, Milner has made him her grandson.

She too is listed in the library files as a shut-in. "I'm all alone," she says. "No brothers, no sisters. I got grandchildren but I don't see them. And every time I see them they got their hand out."

Her place is like all the others: neat, ordered, full of the hallmarks of elderly people; an afghan draped over a chair, knickknacks arranged neatly on shelves, and a TV—always a TV—playing loudly in the background.

Milner, like others along the route, gets a bag filled to the top with books. She can read a whole novel in a single day. There are enough people like her in this complex that the staff started a book club for them. And several use the bookmobile.

"These people are really into their books," says Almira Mathis, senior services coordinator at River Towers. "These are avid readers. They just love to read. Some read a book in two or three days, and that's all they do."

Like many patrons who've grown attached to him, Milner makes small talk with Jacobsen, keeping the conversation going just to keep him around a little while. Then she's satisfied and announces, with mock impatience, that the visit is over. It's Salad Day in the downstairs cafeteria, after all.

"I want you to scat and go to the next place, 'cause I'm going down to the basement where they're having free salad, so skadoodle," she says. "And Aaron, you get your jacket the next time you come."

THE DAY CONTINUES on this way.

During the afternoon, Jacobsen will visit Peggy Ruth Bell, who just had back surgery but insists on showing she can still dance. "Don't I look good for sixty-two? I can drop it like it's hot; I just need a little help getting back up." And she demonstrates.

He'll stop by Otis Carter's apartment, where the gentle eighty-five-year-old simply says, in a wispy voice, "Beautiful. Beautiful" at the sight of bags of fresh books.

He'll drop in on Aretha Hudson, sixty-five, who will come to the door in a housedress and do-rag and will debate him about English royalty centuries ago.

And he'll get several embraces from Theresa Fryer, eighty-six, who grew up in Wales and lived through the Blitz during World War II and will share with him, as she has before, the aloof perspective of someone whose house was hit by a bomb and who lived through it. "If you got a roof over your head, you got clothes on your back, you got food in your house, that's enough," she tells

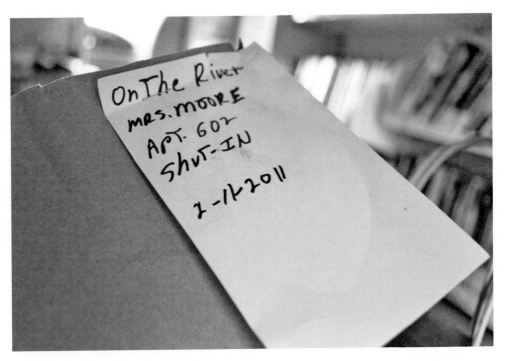

A bag of books waits to be delivered to a shut-in.

him in a still-thick Welsh accent. "All this other stuff is gonna come. You can't worry about it."

After the last stops, as the day winds down, Boyd and Jacobsen head back to their branch in the hulkingly slow bookmobile. Jacobsen reflects on the job.

"It's satisfying, 'cause you do a lot of legwork, you get it done, you sit back with a cup of coffee or just relaxing, going, 'That was a good day.' You meet some big characters. It's just a good day all around."

McCormick says the bookmobile is about more than just the mechanics of bringing books to people. It's why the program has lasted so long, through all the other changes the library's gone through, and why it'll continue. Because there will always be people in the city, some lonely and hiding, who still like having books to read and a familiar person to talk to.

"Books keep people alive, books are friends, they are company," she says. She plans on retiring in a few months but knows she'll still volunteer at the branch from time to time. "We have a lot of seniors in our city who don't have family, and their books serve as their family. That's what they tell us."

Solitary Man

A Homeless Man Finds a Version of Serenity
in the Heart of Detroit

IT'S ANOTHER SPRING morning in Tom Bell's backyard. Birds whistle from the bare branches above, squirrels jump through the crispy leaves below and another day of being alone, another day of nothingness, lies ahead.

Bell is homeless, but only in the official sense. Because when he found this place a decade ago, he made it a real home.

He lives by the river in a tent he pitched atop a tall concrete mound, so high you'd never see him up there if you weren't looking for him.

"I have no phone, no address, no identity either," says the fifty-six-year-old Bell, who's thin, with a shabby beard and a helmet of hair flecked with gray.

His hidden perch is next to a potholed alley, surrounded by a strand of clustered trees and a row of old warehouses left empty years ago. It's a neglected, forgotten corner of the city, one where he can live undisturbed by little else but the sounds of the weather and the animals that share his space. Yet rising from the horizon, just a handful of streets away, are downtown's towering skyscrapers. Bell has managed to find nature's serenity in the heart of the city.

Ten years ago he was living under a freeway overpass. Then, in his wanderings, he came across this mammoth concrete embankment, the remains of an ancient elevated railroad track. He climbed a tree to peek up top, surveyed the strange landscape he found there and decided this was the place for him.

Tom Bell stands in his backyard.

"This is one of the best homeless spots I've ever seen," he says. He went from living in the shadows to basking in the sun, in a world all to himself. And with his find, he claimed one of the most extraordinary places to live a most extraordinary life.

He has no past to dwell on, no future to plan, no job to go to. For him, time is meaningless. The days blend into weeks that become years of sameness, and every moment is the pure essence of now.

"Man, everything's everything," he says. "Ain't nothin' changes. The sun go up, the sun go down. The sun go up, the sun go down. It's what they call just a regular day in the neighborhood."

BELL HAS BEEN homeless since he was eighteen years old. That's almost four decades now. That's most of a lifetime spent living on the streets of Detroit.

"I tried to pay rent, always fell behind payin' rent," he explains. "Never could keep a constant job, never could keep a permanent address, so all that accounts for being relatively known as homeless."

Bell grew up on the west side, he says. But he doesn't like to talk about his life much. He went to high school but says little about that. Doesn't say much about his family, either. He never married.

"I might be what's known as anti-sociable," he says. "If you can't find your kind you can't find your kind. Ain't nothing wrong with that, either. Seldom seen is good, just like all-the-time seen is good. I'm one of those seldom-seen types. I'm always reserved, laid up away somewhere."

Sometimes the only living beings he encounters are the animals living in this grove. He calls them his friends. "They run up and down the trees and all that stuff, raccoons and foxes and cats and different kind of things come up around here. I bring them food to eat, you know."

Four decades outside have taught him the ways of nature and made him intimate with the weather. "I've damaged my feet, close to frostbite. I actually did get frostbit, but it wasn't to the point to where I panicked about it. Some people, man, they actually have to lose it. That ain't good at all. You find out you need your feet and hands."

All those years of experience, though, don't change the fact that it's still hard to live this kind of life. He eats at soup kitchens, collects bottles and cans for the refunds and gets everything else from the trash.

"Being homeless is serious business," he says.

Getting to his place isn't easy. His concrete hill is two-tiered, about fifteen feet high. To get up top he's fashioned a series of ladder steps by nailing slats of wood between two close-standing trees that grow along the concrete wall. Once you climb those there's a braided iron cord that juts out from a crack in the concrete. You grab that to hoist yourself up to the first tier. Then you go up an old stepladder to the top of the second tier. And you're suddenly in his secret world.

He lives on a wide track of weathered old railroad ties stretching far into the distance. They've become smothered in the grasses and tall trees whose roots somehow cleaved the concrete and dug their hold deep. It's like a wild, overgrown park in the sky. "It's perfectly weird," he says.

By contrast, his home is so small he can't stand up inside it.

It's a makeshift tent that's about waist high, shaped like a triangle, made of thin plastic sheeting. He made two round windows fronted by chicken wire, and he fashioned a real wood-framed screen door that latches shut. The top of the tent is shingled with foamy material he found in the trash—one sheet of white, one sheet of black. He cut them into dozens of little semicircles and arranged them in alternating colors, giving it the look of a quaint, miniature cottage.

Once that was done he tamed his landscape. He cleared some grasses, took down a tree or two, defined his yard from the wilds surrounding it. A little garden is guarded by a ceramic frog that watches over the plastic houseplants Bell put in the ground. A birdhouse, detailed and painted, dangles above the garden from a tall, shady tree. A painted woodbin with a hinged lid holds his food, and another smaller one holds his trash.

But his biggest decorative impact was the long mural he painted along the base of his man-made hill. One day he found several half-empty paint cans and some brushes thrown in the trash. He took them home and illuminated the plain gray concrete with a painting that's twenty feet long and five feet high. Split in two by a stenciled image of a chain, the top shows curled black waves against a glowing blue backdrop, while underneath are evenly spaced triangles with different odd designs painted in each. After years of hiding in plain sight, Bell decided to announce his presence here as garishly as he could.

"It was just kind of to let people know that, hey, that's where this one guy who's homeless is. That's all it really is. But I'm not an artist. These are just doodles."

The mural Bell painted at the base of his concrete hill.

IT'S ANOTHER CRISP morning. Bell stands at the foot of his hill, holding a piece of wood. He's building a new place to live at ground level. Too old to climb those makeshift ladder steps anymore, he says. And this time, his home will be tall enough for him to stand up in.

"I've been laying down at home for ten years. I gotta try to get my standing up back where it's supposed to be," he says with a laugh.

But progress is slow. He gets lost in his thoughts easily and will stay in place for hours, watching time unfold around him. This is the pace of his days and the rhythm of the life he's chosen.

"The kind of experience I've had with what's known as convenience or modern, I've had enough of it," he says. "I did the things I'm supposed to do in a house and, well, I don't think that's too much what I'm ready for. Being where I can have peace with myself is what I'm content with," he says. "I'd rather have peace with myself."

He stands there a long while, doing nothing but watching the river, which keeps flowing by, same today as tomorrow, just like this life.

A Second Chance

For One Family, a Business Becomes a Road to Redemption

ARTHUR WILLIS CALLS a customer into the workshop at the back of his store.

"See this?" he says, pointing inside the gears of an old vacuum cleaner. He's showing the man how to perform a minor repair himself for next time. "Tighten this down. There. Now put that belt on that roller." The lesson takes three minutes.

And—with that—he just got rid of some repeat business.

But that gesture, he figures, will bring that customer back for something else some other time. Because here at Bronson's Vacuum Cleaner Service Shop, on McNichols near Greenfield, everything is about helping the customers. It has to be.

"It's tough. Walmart, Sears, I cannot compete with them," says Arthur, fifty-six. "They can sell 'em cheaper, but they can't beat us in service, and that's the benefit of having a ma-and-pa business. Nobody can beat a ma-and-pa in service. They're going to give you the service because they want you back."

The shop belongs to him and his son, Artie, thirty-five. Two longtime employees work here too. The place is a relic from the days before megastores, when a single small business could specialize in a single small item.

When he bought the place twenty-five years ago, it was another shot at having his own business, after his first one was essentially wiped out. But the store became devoted to bigger things.

"It's a selfish reason," Arthur says. "Just to be able to keep a business in Detroit and not sell out. Almost every black business in the city of Detroit is selling out or closing up. We have a tremendous problem with African

Americans in the city of Detroit patronizing African Americans, and our dollars don't stay in the community at all. So our young kids can't get a job."

"What if I can have enough business that I can hire ten of those kids? That means I got ten kids off the street and I'm teaching them a trade. And that's the reason I keep it open, because I refuse to shut it down."

That's not the main reason, though.

ARTHUR ONCE HAD his own janitorial company. His wife ran a maid service.

Things went very well for a while. "We made a lot of money," he says. But he didn't pay all his taxes and it cost him. "You get involved with Uncle Sam in not paying the taxes and he has a way of bringing you down to the bottom," he says. The fines and back taxes ended the good life. Goodbye, Corvette. Goodbye, nice things.

"I was devastated," he says. "You go from having a nice income to no income. But I'm glad I went through it because it's why my faith is stronger. Really, it's not about how much money I make anymore. If I make a lot of money but I'm not happy with anything else, what's the purpose of having the money?"

After his fall, he started going to church more, took Bible studies classes and became a pastor at a church in Romulus. He's also a volunteer chaplain for the Detroit Public Schools. When someone's kid gets shot at school or some other tragedy happens, he's the one who gets the call to come in and comfort the distraught.

Bronson's had been around for years when Arthur found it for sale and bought it. This would be his second chance.

"It never really was mine, though," he says. "This was basically for the family and basically for my son."

All three of Arthur's other kids got college degrees. But Artie didn't want to. Since he was a kid, he'd join his father at work, both at the janitorial company and at Bronson's, watching and learning. Arthur encouraged it. "Because he didn't go to college, I knew down the road that he's gonna need a place to work; he's gonna need this," he says.

Artie (left) and Arthur Willis show off their store's products.

THEIR SHOP IS small. A few dozen vacuum cleaners circle the floor space along the walls and poke upward from shelves standing in the middle. Some are fifty-year-old Hoovers and Kirbys, right next to newer, more elaborate models imported from China. It's like a museum of vacuum cleaner history.

In the old days, they made them heavy and durable, and they'd last for a decade or more. If it broke, you got it repaired. Nowadays they're made of light plastic and break easily.

Bronson's survives because, in tough times, its customers will get their old vacuum cleaners fixed instead of buying new ones, and because, many of them say, the old models are simply better than today's.

"When archaeologists come back a thousand years from now they're still going to find a Kirby," Artie says. "You can burn it, beat it, but you can't break it. They made a model of a vacuum cleaner that actually withstood the test of time."

Most repairs are about twenty dollars. Or you can trade in your old vacuum for credit on a new one. Rebuilt vacuums sell as cheaply as twenty-nine dollars. The vintage models are still popular with the older folks, who know from experience that they don't make them like they used to.

"This one here's probably fifty, sixty years old," Artie says, going into showroom mode. He taps on one. "Everything's cast iron on here. You could go outside and vacuum up the concrete with this. I'm serious!"

He clearly knows his way around vacuums. He had no choice but to learn. This place would become his second chance too.

HE WAS IN his apartment about ten years ago when some guys from the neighborhood broke in and robbed him. He chased them out, called the cops, filed a report. When the police left, the robbers showed up again, and a shootout ensued in the street.

A bullet hit Artie in the leg. He, in turn, shot and killed one of the men. That earned him six years in prison for voluntary manslaughter.

His father had given him the shop and now had to come out of retirement to keep it alive until Artie got out. He'd need it more than ever after this, Arthur figured.

"Coming out of jail is gonna be tough for a young African American to go find a job, 'cause when you get a record or something, it's tough to get a job anywhere, 'cause you get a stigma," Arthur says. "And you see that all over the city of Detroit. Very seldom are you going to make any big money

Arthur Willis shows a customer how to do his own vacuum cleaner repair.

doing anything, 'cause the first thing they're going to ask him is, 'Oh, you did time?' And I didn't want to have the streets be his life."

Artie says he got humbled in prison, sobered up, learned to appreciate the small treasures of a normal life. When he was released, he started a family, started attending church, started rebuilding a life. Now the shop is his again.

"We went in and came out successfully, and we're blessed to still have something to come home to," he says. He refers to himself as "we" when telling the story. So does his dad. They're so close they speak as if they served time together.

Artie tells the story as his young son plays a few feet away. He brings the boy to the shop, just to soak it all in, because he's already planning to pass the place down to him one day, just as his own father did.

When that day comes, it'll be another ring in the ripple a place like this creates. This store gives four people steady jobs. It saved a son from the streets. A young man will grow up and make it his. And a father learned that a family business brings more than money.

"Once you've been successful and once you've lost it and God gives it back to you, it's easier now to live off a little," Arthur says. "You don't need as much as you think you did in the beginning, before you really know why you do what you do. Because before, I was just doing it. But this time around I know why I'm doing it. The value is there."

Plant Life

The Old Packard Factory Sits Abandoned and Crumbling, but It's Home Sweet Home for These Guys

THE TOURISTS WANDERING through their home don't bother them so much. And they're used to the shrill buzz of the saws scrappers bring. Even the snarling bobcat they just ran into in the basement wasn't so scary.

But the people firing guns into the walls have become a bit of a nuisance.

"They just come out here and try out their weapons," says Allan Hill, sixty-five, who points to where a bullet pierced a window, plowed through a ceiling and then kept going to who knows where. "They think that nobody lives here, so they start shooting the building up."

Hill's home is the Packard Plant, the infamous, thirty-five-acre auto factory where production ended a half century ago. He wound up living here after losing a house to a loan he couldn't repay. "I didn't even need to get a loan," he says, ruefully. "I don't know why I got it. But after that, everything started sliding away from me."

He's not a squatter, though. The electricity and water here is paid for each month. He owns the space he lives in. And this is his official, listed address.

A few years ago, a friend with a warehouse at the decaying plant hired him to look after it, and before long Hill moved into one of the little rooms in back. Now it's his.

During days, he started doing side job auto repair on site, fixing cars brought by customers who knew him years ago at garages where he worked. Soon, a few other guys moved in here to live a rugged life in a rent-free space in the middle of nowhere.

They all go by nicknames based on their skills. There's Minister Allan. Mechanic Greg. Carpenter Jeff. Preacher Joe has a house not far down the road but spends most of his time here anyway. And Hill's son Randy just moved in too.

Living in an abandoned factory is as tough as it sounds. "It takes a certain breed of people to handle this kind of stuff," Jeff Lott says.

LIKE ANY FUSSY homeowner, Hill apologizes for the disarray of his place. "Well, it's just a mess right now," he says before reluctantly giving a tour of the living quarters.

He shows the old kitchen, the little bedrooms with mattresses on the floor, the bathrooms and the showers and the big space where a computer on a desk glows in the darkness of a cluttered room. He keeps a website dedicated to the plant and his life here, featuring live rooftop webcams showing what's going on at the factory.

But the main area is the cavernous warehouse. Auto parts blanket the dirt floors, engines dangle from chains beneath the sky-high roof, old car frames and broken-down campers point this way and that. At the center of the metal hurricane are a TV, a stereo, some chairs, plus a set of drums and a couple of guitars they jam on sometimes as they try to coalesce into a band.

Few people are left at the factory besides them. Packard ended production there in 1956, but there were dozens of little companies still operating in the complex until 1997, when the city foreclosed on the property and ordered eighty-seven tenants to leave. Then it was left to rot. The only others left now are a chemical processing company, someone selling exterior lighting, a few squatters now and then and a lot of wild animals.

Besides Hill's dog, a shaggy rottweiler named Baby, they've got a couple of pet raccoons, and they feed lettuce and carrots to a family of rabbits that moved in during the winter. The pheasants that flock around here have provided food in the past. "We do a lot of hunting here," says Lott, forty-seven. "You ever ate city pheasant yet? Oh, it's good eatin'. They're homegrown."

Rats run wild, kept in check only by the several cats Hill keeps or the sharpshooting skills of Lott and fellow tenant Greg Erving, sixty-five. "We shoot rats in here all night," Lott says. They use high-powered pellet guns. "It's a real war going on. You can hear them fighting amongst themselves. Biggest rats in the city. They'll come over and rob your food in a heartbeat. They're bold."

THEY ALL MET one another through one of those grassroots storefront churches that dot the city, the kind that minister to the addicted and the destitute, and their time there inspired them as a group to do something to help those even poorer than they are.

Somehow they became drawn to the bleak Rosebud Sioux Reservation in South Dakota, and for years now the preacher, the carpenter, the mechanic and the minister take road trips to teach the residents there trades like metalwork and carpentry. Unemployment there is persistently more than 80 percent.

"With the hopelessness that they have—they're constantly drinking, everybody's drinking vodka right out of the bottle, there's a lot of diabetes there because of the diet, they need medical care desperately, young people are killing themselves frequently, sometimes it's three or four in one week—with these issues life on the reservation's gotta be hell," Hill says. They pay for the trips with what they earn from fixing people's vehicles.

Hill wants to someday move to the reservation and open a full-time trade school there.

"What am I gonna do with the rest of my life? Am I just gonna stay here, make a few dollars?" he says. "I should go someplace where information and knowledge is appreciated. I'm thinking that if they learn how to do something, you can empower them and they can work off the reservation."

But right now the guys live among plenty of desperate people here. So Hill bought an old shuttle bus, and they began giving rides to the poor and homeless nearby, taking them to obscure little churches, to soup kitchens, to Belle Isle sometimes just to get some air and sunshine.

"It was just put in my heart to do that," Hill says, warming up the shuttle for another day of ferrying poor people around town. "I've found out what a great treasure it is to be able to do that."

TWO DUTCH FILMMAKERS stumble out of the rubble of a fallen building, led by the man Hill calls Preacher Joe. "More like Nightmare Joe," says the preacher. "I'm a nightmare, really."

Either way, he doesn't like to tell anyone his last name. "He's paranoid," Hill says. "He's kind of shy. He thinks that the FBI is after him." Then he laughs. "But maybe they are."

From left: Minister Allan, Mechanic Greg and Carpenter Jeff inside their home at the abandoned Packard Plant.

Joe gives the most colorful and unpredictable tours, and these out-of-towners had the fortune, or misfortune, of stumbling upon him.

"I took them boys all the way down there," says the fifty-two-year-old, pointing down the long street bordered on both sides by the long factory. He loves to mess with people. "They were scared as motherfuckers. They go, 'What is that?' I shine my light down this hole, I go, 'That's where I throw you when you disagree with me.'" He pestered them for cigarettes. Then he suggested they go get beer and leave their camera behind while he watched it for them. They nervously declined. He's been known to ask for "tax" payments from explorers, and he hounds illegal dumpers.

But he's also the one who composed his group's mission statement in flawless prose on a sheet of looseleaf. And he likes the kids who spray paint murals on the walls. He even gives them fresh cans of paint sometimes. "I love 'em," he says. "This is their chalkboard."

Preacher Joe and Mechanic Greg have formed their own band.

From left: Minister Allan, Mechanic Greg, Carpenter Jeff and Preacher Joe outside their collapsing home.

He doesn't live here, but he shares their rough existence. "We ain't got a safe buried up under ground," he says. "We pay electric bills, water bills like anybody else, and it's tight. We're beggin' dog food down here."

They've gotten used to the cold, the solitude, even the concrete buildings that sometimes collapse nearby and shake the ground beneath their feet. They eat dinner together and sometimes watch movies, like any household. But they also get to see the riverfront fireworks from the tall roof, wander a historic warehouse full of things to do and have thirty-five acres of caves and fields and rooftops almost entirely to themselves. Not a bad way to live, Hill notes.

"We've got solitude, no mortgage payment, no credit card," he says. "It's like being in the north woods. Life just goes on, you know?"

The Last Song

Another Mom-and-Pop Record Shop and Community Hub
Closes Its Doors Forever

HE PACKS AWAY the CDs and the old cassettes, leaving the posters on the wall for last.

"I guess maybe it hasn't hit me yet," says fifty-two-year-old Walter Esaw, as he boxes the stock of his little record store, Pearl's Music, on Kercheval near Van Dyke.

But the phone keeps ringing, bringing reminders. "Yes, next week is our last day," he tells each caller who phones him after hearing the news somewhere. "We're gonna be OK," he adds. All the calls are going the same way.

After almost two decades at this spot, and eighty years total in Detroit, the store can't make it anymore.

"It comes down to economics," Esaw says. "The sales are just down. We never were just for profits, but we were always saying that as long as it paid the bills then we would be here."

Business tanked about a year ago, he says. Though the store survived the rise of digital music and the easy-to-find bootlegs in the neighborhood, it couldn't outlast a terrible economy.

For years, Pearl's was a classic corner store on the block, small and old-fashioned, owned by someone in the neighborhood. It specialized in an eclectic collection of jazz, blues, soul and classic R&B—"catalogue" music, as it's called—on vinyl, cassette and CD. The store drew discerning customers and collectors to its narrow aisles, people seeking B-sides and old album tracks and those who didn't want to screw around trying to download obscure old songs using their computers.

"We had a clientele that wanted physical music," Esaw says. "We promoted this to select groups, and they were just loyal customers."

The mail lady walks in the door and brings the day's letters to the counter. "He's not closing," she declares in a defiant tone after overhearing Esaw talk about the store's demise. "He's not going nowhere."

Esaw laughs. "They're all in denial," he says. "I've had customers that came in that I hadn't seen in years saying, 'Why are you guys closing?' I'm like, 'I haven't seen you in years. That's why we're closing.'"

ESAW AND A friend bought the old record shop in 1992, after its longtime owner died and his widow, after whom the store was named, wanted to unload it. "Neither one of us knew anything about the music business," he says. "Of course, we grew up real quick."

He moved the business from its longtime Mount Elliott and Gratiot location to a little brick building just outside Indian Village and worked to make it a comfortable neighborhood place to hang out, hear music, find something rare.

"The first couple years was kind of rough," he says. "We were just looking at making $100 a week just to pay the rent." Every few months they wondered aloud whether to close, but stuck it out. They began attending record conventions, hosting in-store signings, holding promotions for new releases. Eventually, Esaw took over on his own.

Pearl's developed a reputation as a source of hard-to-find music and a go-to stop for touring musicians. Beyoncé was once here, with Destiny's Child, back in their early days. Aaliyah was too, and Toni Braxton, and Usher, and Charlie Wilson and dozens of other famous names.

"I had Trey Songz literally on the floor here, playing jacks with some of the kids," Esaw says. "He sung a cappella, like three songs from on his album, right here on the floor."

The walls are covered with posters and pictures, all autographed, because to get on the wall, whoever's in a picture had to have been in the store at some time.

After the store began doing well, Esaw opened a club in its small basement, named it Pearl's Underground and booked local musicians to play Saturday night gigs.

A jazz set might be followed by blues or hip-hop. Cover was twenty dollars, which bought you a front-row seat to a night of great music and all the liquor you could drink, served from a miniature bar at the back.

It was a tiny club, with room for barely fifty people. There was a scattering of small tables and chairs in front of a short plank of wood serving as the stage. Entrance was invitation only, and you had to pass through three doors just to get in, giving it an air of exclusivity.

It's so legendary on this side of town that after word spread about the basement closing too, customers started offering to hold fundraisers, to at least keep the club open.

"A lot of my customers are saying, 'What are we gonna do with y'all gone?'" he says. "It's been a real outpouring of concern and love."

It's just that it all comes too late.

A LITTLE STORE in the inner city often has a strong relationship with the neighborhood it's in, especially in an area where most of the businesses have closed. Those living in the blocks around it will make a point of shopping there to keep that one alive. A smart store owner knows this and returns the favor.

That's why Esaw would organize customer appreciation block parties with bands, food and games on blocked-off streets. It's why he's taken folks from the neighborhood on bus trips to Cedar Point, with new CDs playing on the stereo the whole way down there. And it's the reason he handed out $1,000 scholarships every year to promising high school students in the city. He'd have them write an essay on a topic like what they'd do if they were president. "We'd sit up at night going through, reading them all," Esaw says.

"It was never about having a record store. We knew that through having a record store, and the music, that we could get kids to come in and talk to us and maybe we could be able to help them do something. We always wanted to do something where we could give something back."

Gestures like these made the neighbors fiercely loyal to Pearl's. Even among the area's thugs, word was to leave this store alone, which sat vulnerable with no bulletproof glass, no anti-theft door alarms, no iron bars on its big windows.

"People in the neighborhood, guys in the neighborhood, the ones that kind of run the neighborhood, they tell everybody, 'Don't mess with Pearl's,' and that all came from a respect thing for all that we did. You never see people come in here with a smoke, you never see someone come in with a drink."

Walter Esaw in front of his record store in its last days.

Once, the store got robbed by an armed gunman. When the neighbors heard what happened, they told Esaw they'd handle it.

"Just to tell you about the neighborhood, two days after we got robbed—they'd taken some cassettes and stuff—they put the money in a cassette with a note saying, 'Sorry we robbed you,' and put it back in the mail chute. I called the police and they said they'd never seen nothing like that before."

Esaw is a full-time accountant, so this job has been a weekend labor of love that started costing too much time and bringing too little money.

"It got to the point I had to reduce my hours, because I was paying someone eighty dollars a day and I was making sixty dollars, so the math don't add up. And if the math don't add up, you got to make a decision."

As he presides over the last days of an eighteen-year dream, music plays from a speaker set on a milk crate outside the door. A sign in the window announces reduced store hours, where before it was a sign warning that the end was near. And the phone keeps ringing, bringing calls from more customers who had to hear it themselves from the owner himself, who has to relay the news, over and over, one customer at a time.

"Music is a luxury," Esaw says, standing behind the store counter, looking through the window at the quiet street outside. "You have to eat, but you don't have to hear some music. Detroit and the state of Michigan are just going through hard times. They just can't afford music anymore."

It's a Man's World

Long-Standing Barbershop Owner Keeps the Old Days Alive

A COP WALKS into a barbershop, and the conversation starts by going downhill.

"Hello, John, how you doing, sir?" the Greek barber asks the Detroit cop. He replies with an unprovoked comment questioning the barber's sexual preferences.

The barber retorts, in so many words, that the cop ought to go have sex with himself. And these two consider themselves friends. "You see how he talk to me?" Pete Kithas, the shop's owner, shouts in mock indignation.

Moments later, two more officers come in, and the conversation is along the same lines. Erections. Hairlines. Oral sex. In other words, the norm here.

Pete's Barber Shop, downtown on Macomb near Beaubien, is an old-time place, the no-frills kind where neighborhood guys used to go to get their hair cut, escape from home for a while, tell some dirty jokes.

Kithas has somehow managed to keep it, in essence if not in exactness, the same as when he opened it in 1962.

The shop leaves little doubt that this is a hangout for the boys. The reading material is the type nobody actually reads: magazines like *Penthouse* and *Playboy* and *Maxim*. The language is locker room. The humor is raunchy.

"It's an old-fashioned barbershop—no kids, no woman, just man," the boisterous seventy-nine-year-old Kithas says in his still-thick Greek accent. "Lots of policemens."

Finding him isn't easy. His shop is on a second floor, up a tall staircase and down a long aisle that runs through Metropolitan Uniform, an eighty-five-year-old police uniform and equipment supply store. There's no door between the two businesses, no wall either. Take two steps and you're out of one place and inside the other. And since the cops shopping for new uniforms find themselves feet away from a barbershop, many have become regulars here.

"You see now, you see those guys, we bullshit a lot," Pete says of the coarse give-and-take. "I come here, I make some money. I have a lot of fun. All my customers over the years are all my friends."

HIS PERSONALITY, HIS life really, is best summed up by a story from his early days.

In the mid-'60s, the three floors above his shop were a flophouse hotel. One day, a man walked upstairs looking for a room but was so drunk the clerk at the front desk wouldn't rent him one. The furious boozer stomped downstairs and threw a temper tantrum on the sidewalk that ended with him kicking in the barbershop's glass door, shattering it.

Kithas was cutting a Detroit Police sergeant's hair when this happened. As the cop heard the crashing glass, he leaped out of the chair and ran outside to confront the large man, who took one swing and knocked the officer out cold on the pavement. Kithas saw this, put down his scissors and stormed outside. Then the drunk took a swing at him too.

Big mistake. Kithas was a Green Beret for Greece in World War II and saw combat in the Greek Civil War afterward. "At that time, they take the best, you know what I mean?" he says, bragging. "You had to be strong. We fight hard."

Suddenly Kithas—thick arms, meaty paws—was face to face with the man who had just kicked in his door, knocked out a cop and threw a punch at him. "The guy tried to hit me," he recalls. "I said, 'You son of a bitch!'" The angry barber punched him once in the face. Lights out.

Two undercover cops parked nearby had witnessed this mayhem, jumped out of their car and ran at Kithas, who had no idea who was now charging at him. So he took one swing, hit a cop in the face and again with one punch knocked a man out cold. Now there were two unconscious policemen on the ground with a knocked-out drunk lying between them.

The sole cop left standing there, stunned at this carnage, pulled a gun on Kithas and screamed at him to freeze. The barber, fists knitted, face flushed, instead started barking back.

"The policemen hit themselves," he told him, audaciously. "I say, 'Why did you not identify yourselves before I hit you? You seen me with my barber

Pete Kithas inside his long-standing barbershop for men.

jacket, you see my door broke, you see the guys down, and he tried to grab me. I don't mean to hit him, but he tried to grab me, so what am I gonna do?'" He was let go.

He's got lots of stories like this, and walls covered with pictures that go with them. One shows him as a young Green Beret. Several are of generals whose hair he's cut. There's one of him with Bill Clinton after Kithas basically talked his way into the Oval Office during a vacation.

"You got to have the guts," he says. "If you don't have the guts, you're dead. You gotta have the guts in everything you do. I don't say, 'I'm sick, I'm not going to work.' Bullshit, I get up no matter what." He brags about shoveling the snow without a hat in freezing weather, just to prove he's still tough.

"My wife says, 'You're crazy.' But I take the cold, I take the heat, it don't bother me," he insists. "Nothing bother me."

WHEN HE CAME to America in the mid-'50s, he set up shop in Greektown, back when it actually was a Greek town, crowded with little stores, butchers, restaurants and immigrants from Greece filling little apartments around Monroe Street.

"They still call it Greektown, they got restaurants, but the casino take over." It killed the historic little district, he says. "They got one coffeehouse. There used to be five, six. And not too many Greeks are left. There used to be a lot of Greeks around here."

In his time, he's gone from a big shop downstairs to a little one upstairs, from three barbers working with him at all hours to cutting hair by himself only during the day. Haircuts are $12.00, a slow rise from the $1.50 they were when he opened four decades ago.

David Silverstein, whose family started Metropolitan Uniform before the Depression, works at the store's counter just feet from the barbershop, and has a front-row seat for the frat party held by Kithas and his customers.

"I have to hear the same stuff over and over day after day," the fifty-nine-year-old says, with mock weariness of the barber's endless stories. "Believe me, I've heard everything." He's known Kithas since the barber first moved to Greektown and Silverstein was a five-year-old dragged to a haircut by his dad.

Kithas listens to Silverstein say these things about him and says, exasperated, "We have argument many times, years and years and years." But then he calls Silverstein his friend anyway.

Between customers, Kithas will sit in his barber's chair, not reading, not talking, just looking forward, relaxing in the enjoyment of being at work still one more day. He doesn't need the money. He just likes the company of the guys.

"My wife say, 'How long you gonna work?' I say, 'Until the day I die.' What's wrong with that? My job is my life," he says. "If I stay home all day I would miss all these people."

After a quiet spell, two more cops make their way in. Two haircuts to be done. And the barber's eyes light up because he sees two more friends.

Custom Revival

An Inner-City Bike Squad Wheels Toward Community in Fallen Neighborhood

ONE HAS A Heineken mini-keg behind the seat. This one has a TV on it. That one has a PlayStation affixed to the back end. Pastel colors glow, polished chrome sparkles.

They're among the dozens of custom bicycles lined along the curb in front of this one house that has no neighbors on either side of it. In fact, just about everything on this street looks drab and depressing. The old houses, the beater cars parked in front of them, the empty lots that sprawl out next to them. Everything except these bikes, which shine like gems in this bleak setting.

They belong to the East Side Riders, a custom bicycle club whose members meet here at what's become their temporary clubhouse on Peter Hunt, an odd little street only a few blocks long near Van Dyke and Harper, deep in the inner city. Club members fish rusty old bikes out of the trash or find frames left curbside and transform them, through painstaking work, into cool, beautiful things.

The club was founded by Dywayne Neeley, now its forty-one-year-old president, and his brother Mike, forty-five. Both men are big and tall; Mike's got thick arms, Dywayne is beefier. They dwarf the bikes they ride.

The club has grown so fast since it began earlier this year that they found a need to write bylaws, create their own Facebook page and implement dues to buy little things like reflectors and host club events. "We're fittin' to set it all up," the president says.

They've done extraordinarily artful and inventive things with the bikes they've rescued. Long, shiny handlebars rise above shoulder height on several of them. Fenders feature fine detailing and lettering with razor-sharp edges. There are trinkets in the spokes and decals on the frames.

Naturally, all these glittering custom rides caught the attention of the kids on the block who were riding around on battered old bikes. Because in a poor neighborhood like this, kids just don't see nice-looking bikes. Certainly none like these.

"Their bikes was raggedy," Mike says. "They didn't have no brakes, they was ridin' around on rims, ridin' on old bikes, so we just said if we can get the parts, we'll just fix the bikes for 'em. That way they can at least ride safe in the neighborhood, they can stop if they have to, they don't be getting hit by no cars out here."

Other kids saw their friends with improved rides, and soon whole groups were showing up in front of this house, sometimes with flat tires to fix, other times just to hang around, watching and learning. In a place where most kids grow up without their dads at home, a yard full of adult men making cool things is a draw for young boys with few role models.

"Normally there'll be like twenty of 'em out here," Dywayne says, looking at the half dozen of them standing shyly on the periphery, staring at the club's bikes. "We got our crew; they got their crew."

When this pack of kids kept returning, they adopted this place and granted the Neeleys their trust, and the brothers felt compelled to look after them a little. "I give them popcorn and cotton candy and I have a big five-gallon thing of Kool-Aid for them," Dywayne says. He has four children of his own. Mike has a daughter too. Sometimes their children are among these kids out front.

Another reason they started hanging out here is because teenagers would chase them away from the portable basketball hoop that's set up a block over. So the Neeleys put a hoop up here so these smaller, younger kids could play unharassed.

"That's some of the stuff we do for 'em," Dywayne says, shrugging. His tone is aloof. It's really not a big deal, he insists. It's just what you do when kids start showing up at your door.

But with those small gestures, their house became the neighborhood's house, and the Neeleys found themselves doing what so many others in so many places in Detroit do. When the area declines, when families fall apart or were never families in the first place, when the city stops fixing the lights or sending the police, sometimes a handful of people will step up to restore a sense of order in little ways here and there that add up to a community.

The Neeleys and their friends just wanted to ride cool bikes. But before they knew what was happening, they were slowly drawn into helping their neighborhood, watching over some of the kids in it and joining volunteer groups they'd never have thought themselves the type to join before.

"You know, it's our neighborhood," Dywayne says. "We gotta do what we can for our neighborhood."

And all of it started because of some old bicycles they made new again.

THE EAST SIDE Riders began with four guys and some dirtbikes they used to get around town.

"Since we was kids, we always was riding bikes over here in this neighborhood," Mike says. "Ridin' 'em, fixin' 'em, buildin' 'em." They'd roll down to concerts at Chene Park or the annual fireworks show on the riverfront and see dozens of guys gathered there on these amazing, tricked-out custom bicycles, grilling food on portable barbecues and watching the show. The sight made Mike's crew and their wheels look sorry by comparison.

"I said, man I can't ride like this no more, I ain't comin' down here like this no more," Mike says. "So I changed my bike. I put handlebars on it, I put shocks on it, put the diamond whitewall tires on it so you could have the cruise, I put everything on it. And we started riding better."

The appeal of a custom bike is putting your own stamp on it, expressing your individuality through it. For years, custom bikes have been part of Latino culture in places like southwest Detroit, where dozens of clubs flourish, but in recent years custom bike clubs have spread to new demographics, like the downriver suburbs and the neighborhoods of Detroit. A big reason is because it doesn't cost much to make one unique. About thirty-five

Above: Brian Goldsmith with a bike that sums it up.

Opposite: The East Side Riders, fronted by eleven-year-old Kaie-la Lee.

dollars for fenders. Maybe seventy-five dollars for handlebars. Another thirty-five dollars for a better seat. A little paint and a lot of patience. "Little thirty-five dollars here, twenty-five dollars there and the bike will come together," Mike says, "But you have to want to put the money in the bike."

The brothers get by nowadays fixing cars and doing home repairs for people and slowly invested what they could into their hobby.

It wasn't just kids drawn to these new creations parked on the street. Some of the Neeleys' adult neighbors, many of whom use bikes as their main transportation, admired how these guys had transformed their rides and formed a club and wanted to join up with them and learn to do the same.

"Everybody saw how we was having fun, going to different little places and riding, and it just grew and grew and grew," Dywayne says. The East Side Riders' membership has risen

Derek and Smooth in the field next to their clubhouse.

quickly; it's about sixty or so now, both men and women, boys and girls, with more asking to join.

Soft-spoken Brian Goldsmith found the club the way it found other custom riders—down at a Chene Park concert, where he was hanging out all alone with his custom bike, admiring this club's amazing wheels. "I purchased my bike a couple years ago," the thirty-two-year-old says. "My bike was a Plain Jane when I first got it, then ever since then I learned how to fix it up." His has yards of chrome, little air horns, big bright headlights, polished mirrors. "My grandmother would kill me if I got a motorcycle," he laughs, "so this is the next best thing." Though he's from a different east side neighborhood, the club liked him and his bike and invited him to join.

With so many now riding in their crew, the Neeleys needed a set of rules for hanging out, to make sure things didn't get loose and unmanageable. When you invest your time and money into something like this, it becomes worth protecting and preserving.

So if they gather or hang out somewhere, the bikers must collect their own trash and take it with them. If the club is barbecuing someplace, the charcoal must be extinguished, bagged and brought home. Bikers have to stay with the pack when they ride and not veer off. If an older member gets tired while riding, the others stop and let him or her rest. And above all, don't start trouble.

"You can't antagonize nobody," Mike says, firmly. "If somebody say something to you out of the way, you say, 'OK,' and keep on going, because we don't carry no weapons or nothing. We ain't trying to be in no trouble. All we trying to do is ride our bikes and have fun."

But then the kids came with their broken-down bikes, looking for help fixing them. Once Mike and Dywayne inadvertently found themselves in the bicycle repair business, they started looking to get a building of their own where they could fix them, teach repair classes and show bikers how to do an orchestrated ride. Problem is they don't have the money. They're hoping for a sponsor or donations or a free space to use.

Most of all they need a clubhouse, one that isn't Dywayne's daughter's home. Right now her house, the one sitting astride a grassy plain with the bikes lined up out front, serves as a storage space for many of their bikes, which are kept inside. They want a fitting place for their club and what it has become.

"It's like a whole 'nother world," Mike says. "I don't even really know how to explain it, 'cause everybody I ran into that's on these bikes that got their bikes hooked up and they come down there, everybody's like family."

THE BODIES STARTED turning up in empty houses and empty lots last year. All women.

When Georgia Johnson learned this was happening where she lives, she was determined to tell her neighbors to watch out for themselves. "Most peoples in the area did not know that eight women, some say eleven, had been murdered," says Johnson, the seventy-four-year-old president of the City Airport Renaissance Association (CARA), a neighborhood group with three decades of history. "So they were shocked. We wanted to get these flyers out to alert the peoples in the community and let them know to be careful."

The bike club gets ready for the long ride downtown.

She typed up a list of common sense safety tips, like "Avoid walking alone" and "If a driver stops to ask directions, avoid getting near the vehicle," and set out to distribute them in her area.

She's been a member of CARA since 1982, its president since 2003. The group exists to pester the city to do the kind of things for the neighborhood it used to do. Fix streetlights. Tear down abandoned homes. Mow the parks. Give grants to poor seniors with leaky roofs. They don't have much luck, she admits.

Her group runs Angel's Night patrols to deter Devil's Night arsons, hands out baskets at Thanksgiving, gives away presents at Christmas. "The city doesn't give us anything," she says. "We are all volunteers, all our money. Whatever we have to do."

But CARA has suffered because its older members have moved on or passed on, and the younger people in this shrinking neighborhood don't seem interested in joining, leaving people like her in charge long after she'd prefer to retire. "I'm a senior and I would love to have a young person come in and fill this void, to fight for the babies and the community, but they seem distant. So that's why we're still here."

In early summer, with the body count rising, she called the local TV stations and newspapers and scheduled a press conference. To show that other residents in this sparsely populated part of town were behind her, she asked the guys she'd seen riding those outlandish bikes to appear in front of the cameras with her, to demonstrate community strength. They were the biggest group she'd seen gathered in the area

"They didn't really have nobody to come out," Mike says. "So they said, 'Bring the bikes up there and we want y'all to represent the neighborhood.'" And the cameras saw the surreal sight of an elderly couple, a handful of concerned residents and a large crew of large men rolling up on these strange bicycles.

Before the East Side Riders showed up, it was left to people such as seventy-nine-year-old William Johnson, Georgia's husband, to slowly walk the long distances between houses and hand out fliers, one at a time.

Instead, the bike club took a stack of them, spread themselves out and covered the streets in a fraction of the time, leaving a copy at each house. Suddenly, CARA had a fast-moving, mobile unit at its disposal. "They were a godsend," Georgia says. She was so thankful, she made everyone in the East Side Riders members of her group. Once again, the bikers were drawn into community service.

Now there was no doubt—the club had transformed into something bigger than before. And it became a point of pride among its members.

"Talk about our charitable work!" several riders implore Mike as he's explaining the role of the club. They're excited about this new dimension to their club.

But they don't really brag about it. They just note it. "We're just some guys, man," Mike says, dismissively. "Basically all we're trying to do is help."

THE STORY OF their east side neighborhood is the same one heard all over the city. How it was a great place once. How something happened. And how it is now.

There used to be houses end to end, they say. The street was full of families. Kids were looked after by all the mothers on the block. And there were fathers around then too.

"When we grew up around here, if I was down the street down there, doin' something wrong and somebody mama came out their house, I was gonna get

it all the way down the block," Mike says. "And then when my mama found out that they got me, she gonna get me again. But it's different now. There's no structure in the home." The guys standing around him nod in agreement. And the stories start to flow.

"The difference that I see from now and then is, when I was coming up as a kid, I wouldn't dare disrespect an adult because the consequences were way too heavy," says Harold Crawford, forty-eight. "And today it's just totally different. It's just really sad that there's not good guidance for the young."

Others say the same thing in different ways. People moved away. Their lingering empty houses made others want to leave too. Soon there were more empty houses than occupied ones, and soon after that there were more empty fields than empty houses. A vicious cycle nobody's yet figured out how to stop.

"Most of the neighborhood is gone," Mike says. "All of the houses. All through that block was full, all of this block was full. You couldn't even cut through this block. You couldn't walk through any fields on this block. And there were more families here."

The Johnsons have figures about their own street to illustrate the decline. "I went counting the houses before this came about, and I counted seventy-five houses," William says. "Now it's about fifteen houses."

That's the backdrop to the sparkling bikes lined up on the street, the backdrop to the childhood of these kids gathered by the house. The Neeleys recognize the difference between their upbringing and what these kids face. They remember others in the neighborhood helping raise them, and as they get older, they suddenly find themselves with the opportunity to do the same, after a band of children showed up at their doorstep one day.

"They see that we're doing something that's cool and they want to emulate what we're doing," he says. "They don't really know what it's all about, but they just wanna be around us."

IT'S SATURDAY EVENING. The kids have scattered or moved on to playing basketball under the hoop in front of the house. The grown-ups are getting ready for another ride to the river. Later that night they'll be a striking sight,

Mike and Dywayne Neeley display their bikes on their street corner.

Women bring their own flavor to the bike club.

moving in sync through the downtown streets. Bus drivers will honk; cops will wave. Mike will lead the pack, wearing a reflective vest, stopping traffic in the intersections, making sure it's safe for his crew to pass through.

Right now, though, he stands next to his bike, with his friends gathered nearby, pausing to think how to explain, even a little to himself, how they all got here, how a few guys with a few rusty bikes got the chance to be better than they were and to make the neighborhood better than it was.

"There's a time in every man's life where it's time out for all the crap and you gotta give something back, you know what I'm saying?" he says. "That's basically what we trying to do. I'm not gonna sit up here, preach to you and tell you I'm a saint, 'cause I ain't. But there's a time for everybody to give something back. And it's my time."

Animal Farm

An Urban Tranquility with Roots in History

A ROOSTER'S CROW cracks the silence and sends the chickens around him scattering in the yard. The only other sound is the faint whoosh of faraway traffic. All around are fields of trees and tall grass with houses in between, but in the background a casino rises above the landscape, a sign that this isn't the country but instead the outskirts of downtown.

Lounging in such rustic serenity is Mary King, an eighty-six-year-old with brittle limbs and a stoop, sitting on her porch and wearing a straw sunhat. Her home and its urban barnyard are in the Briggs neighborhood of North Corktown, one of the city's oldest, a mix of renovated Queen Annes, simple shotgun houses and grass-covered lots. She's got a yard full of chickens on one side of her place and a wide garden on the other, underlining the pastoral look of her surroundings. Her husband died years ago, and her son, who lives next door, takes care of her.

The chickens, more than five dozen of them, give her fresh eggs and meat. The garden, split into neat rows of corn, squash, tomatoes and melons, gives her vegetables for the year. An abandoned apartment building stood there until it was razed, then she took over the plot, removing the brick fragments one at a time by hand until the soil was clear.

With farm life comes farm concerns. Red-tailed hawks perch in the tangled tree above the yard and try to steal her chickens. "They're about as big as a hooting owl," she says. "They'll come down and pick up a chicken in their claws and go up with it." Opossums, too, sneak into the yard for a free meal. And squirrels pilfer from the garden.

The city gave her grief for a time when her chickens would get out and run loose in the streets, but she clipped their wings to keep them home, and now the city leaves her alone.

"That's what keeps me holding on, just thinking about the garden and the chickens and the eggs," she says. "It's so much fun. I don't know nothin' else that makes me more happy."

It wasn't always this idyllic here.

Mary King was the first black person to move into the neighborhood after coming from Alabama in 1948, followed soon by her sister. The locals weren't happy about it. "Oh, we had some trouble 'round here," she says. "When I moved here, they busted out every window in the building. If I could tell you all that happened it would take me two days."

She says neighbors would throw dead rats on the porch. Someone once sent a hearse to the house. She received hate mail. Even a little old lady would taunt her. "She was so old she couldn't hardly stand up; she'd lean into that tree and she'd say, 'Hey, nigger! You old nigger!' She just had veins in her neck and she was calling me nigger. So I didn't do nothin' but smile at her because she was too old for me to hit her. But every time I pass that tree I think about her."

Ku Klux Klan members once detoured from a march to stroll past her new house. She and her sister's husband sat on the roof with a shotgun. "They spied us up there," she says. "They called on us to come back down and talk it out. But they went on their way. They didn't bother us that night."

She stayed through it all. "I would die before I'd leave," she says, still angry about it. "I felt I had just as much right as anybody else to live where I want to live. And that's why I wasn't going to move."

She worked as a maid and an elevator operator until she married and got pregnant with the first of six children and stayed home to raise them. Her white neighbors' rage eventually settled into a slow burn, and their open hostility subsided. Some just moved away, figuring the neighborhood was going to hell. But the resentment had taken its toll.

"I had a hard time," she says. "I had a nervous breakdown. Just about all my hair started coming out of my head in bald spots, you know. I had trouble, but I'm still here and everything is mellow now and I just love it. I'm glad I stayed 'round here. God took care of me, didn't nothin' happen to me. But I could've been killed."

Howard King in the coop with his favorite rooster.

The family had trouble with cops too. One day, her son Howard and some friends were throwing a football around in the street, and the police pulled up. Yelling and shoving led to swinging fists and batons, and three of the four kids were beaten and arrested, according to newspaper accounts at the time.

A white cop broke Howard's hand, used a baton to split his head open over his eye. The fracas would've gone unnoticed if not for the black officer who witnessed and reported it; an ensuing investigation led to a cop's suspension.

A year later, just before the '67 riot, Howard got into a street fight and police were called. They broke down the door of the King house to find him, and Mary wound up in a wrestling match with a cop.

"I was 260 pounds back then," she laughs. "I got him right quick

Mary King watches over her garden.

and I put him on the ground." She grabbed his gun and nearly blew his brains out. "The devil was saying, 'Shoot him! Shoot him!'" she recounts. Instead, Mary got up off the cop. Then she was thrown in the squad car, hit with a baton and bitten in the neck, which required a tetanus shot.

The story spread through the city, and community groups protested in Campus Martius and at police headquarters. Newspapers such as the *Michigan Chronicle* kept the incident alive, and Howard King went from a sports-playing kid to a symbol of police brutality and an icon of the riot's root causes.

Howard was an impressive athlete, tall and thick-shouldered. He even tried out for the Tigers before his life derailed. He served time in prison for second-degree murder but claims he was framed. After parole, he began working with youth organizations. Now, at fifty-nine, he's community director at the

Barnabas Youth Center a few miles away, counseling gang members and kids with lives heading where his once was.

He organizes a community block party every year, confronts drug dealers down on the corner and mows grassy lots on the blocks around his own. "They should give him something for it," Mary says about the city. "If it wasn't for him, this neighborhood would be in a mess."

There's little sign today of the turmoil of the past. The Kings are now elders of the neighborhood where they were once unwelcome. Many houses are gone, and the blocks look more like the Alabama Mary knew and loved—a place where a family can raise chickens without hassle.

"My mother's getting up in her last days, and I believe this is what keeps her looking forward year to year," Howard says. "She looks forward every year to that garden."

She's too old and frail now to garden herself, so instead she sits and watches her son work and basks in days spent, she says, delighting in simple joys brought by little things.

"Sometimes I go out there where my chickens are and go in the fence and sit there and give them a little corn or something, and they be all around me," she says, beaming. "I love that. They start peckin' and I'm just sittin' there lookin' at them. It makes me feel good. It's just beautiful."

Home Free

How an Abandoned Inner-City Apartment Building
Became a Home for One Detroit Family

THE OLD, NARROW apartment complex is ravaged. Curtains blow out of broken windows and weeds smother its courtyard. All signs point to its abandonment.

But there's a handful of colorful toys scattered on the porch outside one of the back doors, which faces a long, empty field. And clothes hang on a line to dry. Amazingly, despite the squalor, someone still lives here.

It's home to the Tipton family—Rick, his partner Jennifer Coombs and their three daughters. They occupy No. 1909 in the crumbling Spaulding Court apartments on Rosa Parks Boulevard at Spruce.

They live here for free because their landlord abandoned his own building and left the place to the scrappers and vandals who moved in as the tenants moved out. The family, broke and struggling, stayed.

"If you want to get technical, we're basically squatting," Rick says. "It has helped us out financially, but we can't live like this anymore."

Their apartment has electricity still, but they had to rig up their own water supply after the building's old pipes were stolen. They don't have jobs. They don't own a vehicle. They do a lot of walking to get around.

Rick, thirty-eight, has a wiry build, a shaved head and a nagging criminal record. After years spent on Skid Row and in prison, he's trying to lead a respectable life and be a good family man while stuck in a bad situation.

The Tipton family on the steps of the empty building where they stay.

Mom and daughter inside their kitchen.

It's a summer morning, and he's smoking a cigarette in a shaded area near the porch. One of his daughters rides her bike back and forth in the narrow, sunny space where the kids are allowed to play. Jennifer watches from an open window. The girls are never let out of sight except for school and aren't allowed to talk to the strangers who pass by or cut through here.

"I make sure that my kids have everything they need," Rick says. "My kids don't want for nothing. They're fed every day, they have clean clothes. We make sacrifices to give them that."

Jennifer brings Kyrstyn, eleven, from a previous relationship. Rick does likewise with Darian, eight. Little three-year-old Dallas is theirs. The girls are polite, friendly, quick to smile and well behaved, a surprise considering how the odds are stacked. The oldest daughter has lived elsewhere and remembers there's a better life out there. For the youngest two, though, this has been home much of their lives. And until they get back on track, back to a normal life, the couple hopes to keep the kids from being ruined by their time here.

"We take them to the water park, they go to the zoo, we treat them like any other children," Rick says. "They're very well adjusted. They don't realize they're in a situation not like other kids, and I don't want them to ever have to feel like they're any lower than anybody else."

WHEN THEY MOVED in a few years ago, Spaulding Court was a nice place to live, featuring two sleek wings, walls of cut-stone blocks and a courtyard through the middle. Each pair of apartments shared a covered porch capped with a brick archway. They'd been solid for a century. All twenty units were occupied.

Then the landlord stopped showing up to collect rent or to perform maintenance. A couple years later, he returned to serve eviction notices. And then he vanished, again.

As the place fell apart, its residents left one by one. Empty apartments were ransacked. Windows were shattered. Doors were kicked in. A couple units got torched.

The family had nowhere to go and no money to get out. For a while they attempted to contact the landlord, first for repairs and then just to learn what happened, but his last known phone number is disconnected, and his last address was a box at the post office.

Meanwhile, they live in a nearly abandoned building. Scrappers break down the doors to empty units and tear out anything that's metal. Drug dealers moved into the vacant unit across from the family a while back and set up shop until Rick chased them off. Amateur photographers sometimes wander the ruins until they hear him barking at them from a window to get the hell out.

"I don't come to your house with cameras and take pictures of your house," Rick says. "We might not be living in a mansion in Bloomfield Hills, but this is still our home, and don't invade my home."

The apartments are such bleak symbols of decay that when Eminem was shooting a video this summer for "Beautiful," featuring images of the city's abandonment, his crew wandered into this place and put in it a brief shot of Jennifer and Dallas sitting on their back porch, next to a slack utility wire.

"I'm getting phone calls from everybody I know, saying, 'Your daughter and your wife's in the video!'" Rick says. They like Eminem. They were proud to be featured. Now their time here is immortalized.

The littlest girl: Dallas peers into the doorway of the abandoned apartment next door.

Spaulding Court was abandoned by
its owner and ravaged by scrappers.

RICK'S LIVED A hard life. He grew up in the Cass Corridor. "My mother was a heroin addict, my dad was a cokehead and my sister was a stripper," he says. "So that was a way of life." He did drugs and sold drugs, used a gun to rob someone and was sent to prison. He got out, assaulted someone and was sent back again.

He swears he's a new man since his release, but he can't find work because few employers are eager to hire a felon, particularly when the economy has tanked. He is, despite his life on the streets, a trained chef and worked in a few respectable restaurants around town before being sent away.

"I've put in applications everywhere I could think of," he says. "Now it's hard for me to get a job in a nice restaurant because of my record, because it's a violent thing. But if somebody would just give me one chance, let me get my foot in the door, I'm not that kid anymore. I was twenty-one years old. I was crazy. I'm not that person anymore, but they don't see it that way."

Father and daughter: Darian and Rick Tipton at their dining room table. Lunch that day would be a five-dollar pizza.

He and Jennifer met through friends a few years back. She had come north from a small town in Ohio when her mom remarried and moved here. She and Rick dated, and he moved into the apartment. Then she hurt her back and couldn't work anymore. Surgery didn't help. That left them with state assistance checks, cash from odd jobs and few options as Rick tried to make it the respectable way. It's hard to do, he admits.

"We were talking the other day. I said, 'You know, I can go out here and in a week I can get us out of this situation,'" he says, referring to old friends still deep in the drug business. "'Get us a nice house, a nice car. Just give me one week,' and she says, 'Hell no.'"

They're an odd pair, opposites who find in each other something they were missing in themselves. She's a polite girl from the country; he's a reformed ex-con from the city streets. She grounds him; he protects her. Right now, all they have is each other and the kids.

Jennifer peers out from the living room to the empty courtyard outside.

"I'll go do something stupid and she'll say, 'Normal people don't think like that,'" he says. "I get so frustrated, I do slip back into that frame of mind, and then I turn around, I look at her, I look at my girls and I go, 'What kind of future would they have if I go ahead and do something stupid again?' Not that I probably would do it, but she keeps me in line." The couple plans on marrying in the fall, a gesture toward their ideal of traditional family and a normal life.

THE BENEFITS OF living rent-free were long ago outweighed by the building's disrepair. "I hate this place with the biggest passion in the world," Jennifer says. "I cannot stand it." She aspires to one day move someplace Downriver, like Melvindale.

The girls primp in the mirror.

As she talks, Darian rides her bike back to the porch to make her chief complaint about living here. "I don't have a TV in my bedroom," she says. And then she beams, a pure, beautiful smile. If she or her sisters are somehow hardened by their time here, it's not obvious.

Just days later, the pieces come together—Jennifer's disability checks begin arriving, Rick lands just enough odd jobs and an apartment becomes available down the street. It's nothing special, but it's clean and secure, and it's available just before fall.

It puts them a few weeks closer to surrendering Spaulding Court to the vandals and vagrants. A few weeks closer to a more normal life.

"Our goal is, we want to give them a better shot than we had," Rick says. "Me, growing up, I had to fight and scrape for everything I had. I don't want it to happen to them."

Opposite: Jennifer and Darian on the stoop of their apartment, seen through the abandoned building across the courtyard.

The Candy Man

Old-Fashioned Party Store Keeps It Simple

"HOW YOU DOING, young fella!" shouts a jolly Mr. Boyd to the little kid standing at his store's counter. The boy, probably about seven years old, asks for a pack of gum. "Oh you're gonna be doing some chewin', huh?" Boyd replies enthusiastically. He gives him the gum and lets the kid owe him a nickel. He's the only customer this hour.

This is how the days usually go at Boyd's Party Store, which sits in the middle of an east side neighborhood at the corner of Moran and Hancock. The place is old and spare, like a little country store, set among patchwork houses and prairie lots.

It belongs to Neal Boyd, soon to be seventy-three years old. He's known by his customers simply as Mr. Boyd, an indication of the respect he's accorded by everyone around here.

"I'm a father figure or a grandfather figure, and some of them just look at me as a good fellow," he says. "Most of the people around here respect me and I respect them too. There's been a lot of folks I've helped."

You'd never know the store was here unless you're right up on it. Two small, hand-painted signs nailed to its mint-green aluminum siding are all that set it apart from the other houses on the street. Built more than one hundred years ago, it's a wood-frame building attached to a house, the kind common then, when proprietors lived above or next door to their businesses. Instead, there's a landlady nearly as old as the store living in the house attached to it. Boyd looks out for her, doing small repairs as the house ages.

Nowadays, customers are usually either children buying candy or adults buying beer, one tall can at a time. Both sets of customers pay with pocket change.

"I ain't doing much business, I'm gonna tell you like it is," he says. "It's slow, man. I like to be busy, at least like to be ringing the cash register."

It's small inside there, with just a few stand-alone shelves holding the bare-bones basics—bread, bologna, chips, some frozen microwaveable meals—just enough food to qualify with the state to accept food-assistance cards from his customers. The glass-door coolers offer pop, plastic pints of fruit juice and single cans of cheap beer like Milwaukee's Best, his bestseller at $1.50 each. Behind the counter are boxes of candy and gum for the kids, and rolling papers and cigarettes for the grown-ups.

There's an old exhaust fan above the door, and ceiling fans that make a small breeze, but in the summer it gets hot as hell in there, and Boyd will sit out on the stoop out front and talk to passersby until someone needs something inside—little kids wanting treats, adults thirsting for beer or begging for food.

"'Mr. Boyd, I'm hungry. I need some food until Wednesday,'" he says, imitating a customer, "and that's been two months ago. So he got fifteen dollars worth of stuff, 'cause I ain't gonna let you leave out of here hungry. I ain't seen him since. He lives around here too. I think what he really want to do was sell it and get some drugs. Probably need some drugs for himself."

Boyd came to Detroit from the Mississippi Delta in 1959, leaving behind a dead country town. "There wasn't no jobs," he says. "All there was down there was cotton fields and cornfields back then, so peoples come to get a better job." He went into construction, raised nine children and a couple of decades ago passed the old party store, found it for sale and took over from the old Polish owner.

Over the years, residents moved out in waves, and now it's mostly poor people left in the neighborhood. "It's just terrible right now," he says. "It's bad right now. People just ain't got nothin'. It's terrible."

One neighbor even taught him how he traps and eats the wild pheasants darting around the fields here—get a stovepipe, put screen on one end of it and put feed inside. The dumb, hapless bird walks in there to eat and gets stuck. "He go in there and eat but he can't turn around, 'cause he don't know how to back out," he says. "We got plenty pheasants here in the city. Sometimes I sure would like to have them in the skillet."

Someone who couldn't afford utilities inadvertently blew their house up a few months back, just one street over. "Yeah, shit, it blew windows out of houses over here. It was a mess. Somebody was stealing gas. We thought we'd been hit with a bomb." These are the snapshots Mr. Boyd offers to describe life around the neighborhood now.

Despite life's hardships out here, Boyd glows with enthusiasm when children come in. He sees through the "street" personas they've picked up and senses the innocence still in them. Even the kids who've developed foul mouths and sticky fingers still meekly request sweets. He'll sell candy at a loss to them, give the poor kids free samples and if one child has money but his friend doesn't, he'll give both of them the same number of pieces. In exchange, he turns most interactions into lessons he hopes will counteract bad behaviors they've learned.

"My main thing is telling them to stay away from the drugs and stuff and treat people the way you want to be treated," he says. "I tell them you can do whatever you want to do if you put your mind to it. I've had a lot of them that had left here and turn out to be real good, and they come back and thank me. Then I've seen some that I know who was young that look older than me because they out there on them drugs."

Boyd keeps the leisurely hours of one o'clock in the afternoon to ten o'clock at night, most of it spent on his stool, behind bulletproof glass. The old coolers chug along as he waits; otherwise, it's dead quiet but for the crickets in the fields and the sound of children sometimes playing outside in the street.

The road out front is still spotted with houses, but on the side streets behind it, the empty fields are growing in number.

"They been saying they gonna come through and buy all this stuff and rebuild," Boyd says. "I bet they can with all these vacant lots and stuff, but so far they've been saying that for a while. I don't see nothin' yet, though."

Sometimes customers come in to just say hi to the man who actually had a hand in bringing them up. "I know practically everybody that come in here," he says. "Even if I don't know them, they know me; they know me 'cause they done growed up and I don't know them because their face changed a little bit."

With so few customers, he mostly works just to pay the bills, to break even and keep the store open. "Me, I drink," Boyd says, frankly, contrasting himself to the unemployed drinkers scrimping change to buy single beers in the daytime. "I'll have a drink but I know when to drink. If I need to buy some stock and I just got enough money for stock, I ain't buying no liquor."

And then he leans forward, his words take a sentimental tone. "I call the store my woman. If she needs something, I got to put it in here, 'cause I know once I open that door somebody gonna come in here and buy something, but if I ain't got it I can't sell it. Gotta take care of her first."

Mr. Boyd leans back and waits for customers at his little convenience store.

Labor of Love

Inner-City Repair Shop Hangs on Reasons Big and Small

A PINK BLOOM climbs a windowpane and leans softly against the cold glass. It shouldn't be here at all, in late winter, hanging heavy on a thin stem. Yet it's one of a handful of improbable flowers crowding the front window with a dozen other potted plants at Lip-Pan TV, on the corner of Chene and East Warren.

Tom Reynolds, the gray-haired and mild-mannered owner of the shop, is the gardener, the one who draws blooms from a plant that should be dormant this time of year. "They were my wife's," he says. "We usually had them outside at home. I used to bring them here in the winter. I take care of them."

The plants hold more meaning now than in years past because his wife, Gloria, died of cancer a few months ago at sixty-four. They're now a living link to his missing half, so he takes painstaking care of them. "I was with her for fifty years," the sixty-six-year-old says softly. "I have a lot of good memories. We did a lot together."

The window flowers, behind protective metal bars, contrast with the hard circuits and cold tubes that stock shelves and fill boxes at Lip-Pan, a repair shop for TVs, DVD players, VCRs and stereo components. The place is located on the wasteland that is Chene Street, once the commercial artery that connected Polish neighborhoods in Detroit to those in Hamtramck, before nearly everyone left and the area crumbled.

"People got scared," Reynolds says. "They really did. A lot of things changed." The destruction of a neighborhood to make way for the General Motors Detroit-Hamtramck Assembly plant in 1981 was the deathblow to an area battered by urban renewal schemes, new freeways and white flight.

Tom Reynolds (left) and Jim Dalton keep many things alive at Lip-Pan TV.

"Once they cut off Chene Street, people didn't want to go around that thing," he says, referring to the auto plant and the winding road around it. "GM said, 'Oh, we're gonna do everything for the neighborhood, we're gonna help you.' They didn't do shit. Nothing. It's really a shame because it was a nice neighborhood. Maybe it still would've went down, but that made it start faster."

The project razed thirteen hundred homes, 140 businesses, six churches and a hospital to make room for the auto plant. "When General Motors has all these problems, it doesn't bother me," Reynolds says, bitterly. "After what they did to this neighborhood, I don't care what ever happens to General Motors. What goes around comes around."

Lip-Pan is one of the few operating businesses left on Chene. "There used to be one on every block," he says. "The guy who ran this before used to belong to a business association, and there were like eight hundred businesses they represented."

The shop opened in 1948, christened Lipan after an original owner. Over the years, an extra "p" and a hyphen somehow crept into the name. "It's a stupid name," Reynolds says, "but people remember it." He began working here when he was nineteen and eventually took over.

It's in one of those old, long buildings common in the city, a narrow rectangle that stretches far back from the small front lobby and counter. Such buildings used to be stacked next to one another—from one end of a block to the other—all over town, but now you often see one or two standing alone, like a single tooth in an otherwise toothless mouth.

Their workshop is stacked with hundreds of TV and stereo components, organized loosely, poking out of boxes haphazardly, on shelf after shelf.

Years ago the shop had a building connected to it until someone tried to break in by setting its wood front door on fire. The blaze destroyed the edifice and jumped atop Lip-Pan, scorching the upstairs apartment, rendering it uninhabitable.

The '67 riots inflicted more damage. Reynolds credits nearby residents with saving the shop. "When they had the riots they broke all the windows, but it was all the people in the neighborhood that protected this place," Reynolds says. "They stayed in here. They watched so nobody would do anything."

The front door swings open regularly, bringing in someone picking up or dropping off his broken TV or dusty old radio. Customers usually live in the neighborhood or did at one time. Besides doing repairs, Lip-Pan also sells phonograph needles, refurbished TVs and radios and parts like circuit boards and TV tubes. Sometimes people wait in the lobby for the bus; Reynolds lets them sit inside during the colder months.

Jim Dalton, the only other employee here, notes a peculiar phenomenon—the old people in the neighborhood yearn for music as winter retreats and come here with their broken turntables. "In the spring they want to play their records," the sixty-four-year-old Dalton says. "All year long they don't mess with them records, but in the spring, when it gets warm weather, they get their old records out."

The pair's van is emblazoned with the shop's logo, but they don't make house calls anymore. "You don't know whose house you're going into sometimes nowadays," Dalton says. "You go to make the delivery and then they start an argument with you. They don't want to pay. Then they got a whole bunch of people outside and you're scared. What can you do? You can't take the TV out with all those guys out there."

They've had a couple holdups, but neither man has been hurt. "You get a cold chill, like somebody's walking around on your grave," Dalton says about having a gun pointed at him. "For about three months I was nervous afterwards. Anybody that comes in with their hand in their pocket you think they're holding you up. But it fades after a while."

Though Reynolds could retire—"I just got my first Social Security check"—he keeps the shop open, partly out of habit, partly to sustain something familiar. He isn't given to demonstrations of sadness, but his sentimental acts say everything about the hole in his life. People sometimes stop in and ask to buy one of the plants in the window. "I just say, 'Nah,'" he says. They have too much meaning now.

Gloria's fingerprints are still here and there in the shop. She used to work here, doing the books, answering the phone, the "dirty work" as Reynolds calls it. The old bathroom is decorated with a little vase she put on the toilet tank with dried flowers poking out and a couple of small nature photos on the wall, a charming, feminine touch in a room too dingy for it to matter.

And Reynolds still wears his wedding band. "I've never had it off," he says. "Never. I don't even know it's on anymore." The ring shows his is a love interrupted by death but not diminished by it.

The shop, the ring, the plants, all link to what once was an attempt to hang onto some aspect of what's gone—a loved one, a wrecked neighborhood, an old shop. "There's a lot of good people around here," Reynolds says, looking outside. "That's what keeps everything going, what's left."

It's usually quiet inside, between customer visits, as the two men busy themselves fixing broken things, and a missing love is remembered in lovely little gestures and in plants kept alive by a heartbroken gardener.

Down by Law

Old-School Bodybuilder Takes on the FDA and Loses

IT'S NOT THE same anymore for Ron Kosloff. Not since they came after him, ruined his livelihood, broke his spirit.

"They don't like me," he says, ominously.

They are the Food and Drug Administration. And several years back, they paid him a series of unpleasant visits from which Kosloff still hasn't recovered, financially or emotionally. Suddenly he pauses and says nervously, "Please don't get me in trouble."

Kosloff, seventy-two, is gentle and soft-spoken, a big man with a graceful walk. He's owned Research Nutrition on Seven Mile near Hayes on the city's east side since 1974, selling products based on what he calls "old-time bodybuilding," the workouts and diets that were made famous in the 1940s and '50s by fitness icon Vince Gironda, Kosloff's idol.

The store sells oddities like dried bee pollen and glandular extracts, chlorine shower filters and reprinted pamphlets describing years-old exercise techniques. Kosloff's against most prescription drugs and believes good nutrition can prevent or cure most physical ailments. Diabetics come to him for pancreas extracts, and alcoholics come to him for liver pills. Both believe the supplements will regenerate their poor, punished organs.

The store is nestled in a small strip of storefronts, hard to spot if you're not looking for it. Open the front door and you're in a tiny, dim lobby with a small counter. The nutrition products he sells are stacked in a storeroom in the back. There's no showroom to browse. Most of his sales nowadays are by mail anyway, ordered online.

Kosloff admits he's an eccentric. "I'm a little bit different," he says. He detests sugar and iodized salt and says fiber is actually bad for you. He thinks all pro athletes are on steroids. And he doesn't believe in calorie counting. Or calories, for that matter.

"There's no such thing as calories," he says. "That's a fabricated theory. Calories is the amount of heat needed to raise one gram of water one degree Fahrenheit. What's that got to do with losing weight? It's got nothing to do with losing weight, but our society has turned into a society where lies are told to make money."

It's a recurring theme with him. Madison Avenue and big corporations, he insists, have brainwashed us, told us to eat carbs and drink sugary pop and kill ourselves just to make themselves rich. They're against nutrition and vitamins because they need us to be sick so we'll have to pay costly visits to the pharmacy.

"The medical profession spends zillions of dollars every day hawking drugs," he says. "They don't want to talk about the holistic way. They want to talk about drugs. It's only the intellectual who's going to say, 'This is not right.'"

Kosloff's the author of dozens of articles espousing these convictions. They're on his store's website, with titles like "Grains: The Great Coverup of an Insidious Sickness" and "The Coming Conspiracy of a Planned Pharmaceutical Menace." The FDA was one of his favorite targets.

Little did he know when he wrote those things that the FDA would one day show up at his door.

KOSLOFF GREW UP scrawny and took up bodybuilding to change that.

"I was skinny and I didn't have that much going for me," he says. "I just wanted to look better, just so people wouldn't pick on me, and naturally if a girl looks your way that's a little helpful."

And that's when he first set eyes on Vince Gironda. Back in the 1950s and '60s, Gironda was an iconic bodybuilder. He'd operated the famous Vince's Gym in Hollywood since just after World War II. Movie stars flocked to him for training. They called him "the Iron Guru."

Gironda was unorthodox and became more so as his life went on. He was opposed to training abdominal muscles at all. He drank raw milk and suggested eating three dozen fertile hen eggs every day. He claimed kelp pills help increase muscle definition. But mostly he preached against steroids. The natural way, he declared, is the only way.

Ron Kosloff with a picture of Vince Gironda, his idol.

He was temperamental and would suddenly throw someone out of his gym if he thought they were doing an exercise incorrectly. When a young Arnold Schwarzenegger visited him, Gironda told him he was a "fat fuck" just because he hated arrogant celebrities.

Kosloff was so impressed by Gironda that he got him on the phone, made an appointment to see him, flew from Detroit out to California and wound up staying there for six weeks for one-on-one training. They became lifelong friends.

But in the '80s, modern fitness centers sprouted up everywhere, and suddenly Vince's Gym seemed old-fashioned. It closed in the '90s, and Gironda died a broke and broken man, soothing himself with the bottle until his last days.

Kosloff still looks up to him, even in death. There are photos of Gironda, posing or flexing, framed and hung on the walls throughout his store. Gironda's pamphlets on diets and workouts are neatly arranged on display at the front counter. And when Kosloff speaks of him, his tone is flush with affection.

"Nobody had definition like he did. I mean, he was just a phenomenal man. If you read those articles that I wrote about him you'll see what a great, great man he was."

Today, Kosloff is the keeper of Gironda's legacy. He sells his workout courses, lives his advice, sells the products his mentor helped formulate. His answering machine fills every day with calls from such places as Hawaii and Delaware, England and Canada.

"It's still a cult," he says. "All the people that call me, they embrace Vince Gironda, they embrace old-time bodybuilding. But he was attacked viciously for the things he preached."

In a way, he likes to note, he's now suffered the same unfair fate as his hero.

THE INFANT FORMULA in the stores offers poor nutrition, Kosloff says. "Babies are being fed garbage." So eight years ago, he came up with his own blend, packaged it and sold it.

Kosloff says he heard that a woman found his formula on a local health food store's shelf, fed it to her baby and was so impressed by the results that she went to her doctor and cheerfully told him all about this new product, adding that she wasn't coming back for the doctor's own treatments for the baby's digestive problems. The doctor called the FDA. And the agency brought the hammer down.

In early 2004, a warning letter became a phone call that became a knock on the door, and Kosloff soon found himself pouring out can after can of his formula under their watchful gaze. He lost a fortune.

"It was devastating," Kosloff says, his eyes welling with tears. He would've retired by now, he says, if it weren't for the financial hit he took.

The agency never said his formula was harmful, only that he didn't notify them about his new product and that he mislabeled it as food rather than merely a dietary supplement.

Patricia El-Hinnawy, FDA public affairs officer, acknowledged the agency's actions against Kosloff but would note only that, in general, the "FDA can recall infant formula if it determines that the product is adulterated or misbranded and therefore presents a risk to human health."

So Kosloff fell back to selling his liver pills and enzymes, taking phone calls from faraway gyms, counseling people on what they eat, keeping a low profile.

But it's just not the same. He sits in his chair with a slump of defeat, his voice a sleepy whisper, his face that of a man looking over his shoulder.

"These aren't good times," he says. "I'm just carrying on. See, you don't fight big corporations. I realized what power was." He's convinced the FDA will come after him if he talks about this. Still, he talks anyway.

He has a picture of himself standing arm-in-arm with his idol on a cloudy day long ago. It shows two men tied through the years by their shared beliefs, the feeling of being alone in their truth and the sense that you just can't fight the power.

"I'm just another Vince Gironda," Kosloff says. "You tell the truth, and they'll get you. The truth in America doesn't fly. Everything is just bullshit. It's sad."

Dirty Dancing

Detroit Strip Club Battles Its Own Checkered Path to Fix Its Image

THE COPS DON'T believe him. Neither do some customers. But H.B. Lawrence, the manager of the All Star Gentleman's Club on Eight Mile, is determined to prove that his strip club is now clean.

He took it over a few years ago, back when the place was notorious for fights, clouds of weed smoke floating in the bar and lap dances with limitless extras. It had nicknames like "The Death Trap" and "Fight City," reflecting its confined space and the mayhem that took place in there. Police showed up all the time.

"Previous management thought they needed your business," Lawrence says, "so if you poured Champagne on the floor, it's acceptable. If you struck one of my entertainers, it was acceptable. If you roll weed right on the table and smoke it, that's acceptable. Well, we don't do that here anymore."

All Star is, as the euphemism goes, an "urban" strip club, where most of the customers and strippers are black. The forty-four-year-old Lawrence has been trying to shift its status from low-end to high-end adult entertainment, trading thug life for high life, marketing the place as upscale and betting that showy can outdraw sleazy.

"When you come here, we get you caught up in it, you get so lost you don't know what hit you," he says. "We go faster and harder here than anywhere else. You leave and go, 'I'm broke as a motherfucker, but I had fun, though.' That's all that counts to me. You're probably not going to remember what happened to you the next day. We're Ringling Brothers. It's a circus."

LAWRENCE IS THE ringmaster. He's the one who bosses the strippers, watches the door and makes sure the money flows in. His initials are short for DJ Hard Body, the name he had for years while spinning records at strip clubs around town. Before that, he was a male stripper. Between the two jobs, he's spent twenty years in more than twenty clubs learning how the business works.

He was a DJ at All Star for years before convincing the owners to pour a quarter-million dollars into its renovation—a gamble to convert a ghetto dive into a glitzy club. They made him general manager.

First thing he did was ban pot smoking in the bar. Then he tore down the VIP wall, turning what was essentially brothel space into a display area with little privacy. Next, he ruthlessly culled the crew of strippers.

"When the bar went upscale, I had to let go a lot of girls I really care about because they'd gotten on in years, gained thirty to forty pounds, thirty-three years old now," he says. "In the old days you had a little longevity dancing. Now you burn up a girl in a few years."

He outfitted the bouncers and the valet staff with earpieces and walkie-talkies, coordinating who gets thrown out or invited inside. "Lots of things let you know not to let somebody in," he says. "Twelve guys wearing white T-shirts with the dead guy on their T-shirt and they just came from his funeral—uh-uh, you're not coming in here, baby, 'cause I know what happens. They want to grieve, and 'grieve' means pouring alcohol on the floor and slapping girls around."

Old customers got tossed from the new All Star or were refused entry. "The smoking weed, the smacking girls, the standing up and tearing up the bar—these guys watch too many fucking gangster movies and too many rap videos," Lawrence says. One by one troublemakers got banned, and enemies were made of those who sometimes settle disputes with guns.

"A lot of guys feel that you disrespect them when you ask them to leave the club or put them outside," he says. "So guys will run around that fence, that brick wall and drive by and fire at the bar, and whoever's in the way is in the way." Lawrence says customers standing in line have been shot. His cousin took a bullet in the jaw while standing in the parking lot. Some people are still angry at being banned from their favorite strip club— a reason Lawrence goes by his DJ name.

H.B. Lawrence on stage with several of the All Star dancers.

The stage is narrow and the space is small.

The dancers say they're relieved the thug element has been reduced if not entirely eliminated. "They'd come in and get dances and walk out and not pay you," says twenty-seven-year-old Creamy, a veteran here. "They were experiencing their rough times in life and was taking it out on the girls. Nobody was making any money on the streets. Everybody was angry."

The customers eventually realized things had changed. But not the cops. As a result, there were many vice squad raids here, even after the makeover. The club's lawyers sued not only the police but also the city over local laws such as the requirement that strippers pay for "dance cards" in order to work, which empowered such raids. Several lawsuits were filed; a few still sit in the courts. A federal judge sided with the club last month and issued an injunction that prevents any more raids at All Star until all the lawsuits are settled. Yvette Walker of the Detroit Police Department's Public Information Office referred questions about the raids and the lawsuits to the city's Law Department, where several messages were left and not returned.

Through all this, Lawrence took another tack and launched a public relations effort, speaking at a nearby church meeting held to protest the club and meeting with cops to make his case that if it's possible to have a respectable strip joint, All Star is it.

"Customers and police, if you've been in here in the last two years, you absolutely know it. Now, whether you accept it or not, that's on you. You get guys who won't let go of the old All Star, though."

It's THREE O'CLOCK in the afternoon on a Saturday, and most seats in the All Star club are filled. A thin, sharp-dressed loner sits on a barstool and pulls out a thick wad of twenty-dollar bills to dispense. He lets it linger in the open, just holding it, showing it off. Next to the stage, two guys eat fried food and watch the dancers passively. Others drink expensive liquor or smoke cigars and ask for stacks of singles so they can make it rain on a dancer. One-dollar bills are scattered everywhere—on the stage, across the floor, in the seats.

These new customers, Lawrence notes, don't come here to get high or get laid. They come to get noticed. "Guys come here to see and be seen, to flash, throw money in here," he says. "They want you to see it. They're like, 'I'm the boss.'" He claims some customers go to lower-end strip clubs to get off in their private, anything-goes VIP sections, then come to All Star to relax and drink and play the part of a high roller.

They are given a spectacle. Lawrence is a showman, a natural promoter who puts videos from the club on YouTube, distributes fliers around town featuring pictures of his club's strippers and even stages Sunday boxing matches between the girls, with a ring set on the stage in which two dancers in bikinis swing wild, gloved punches at each other, sometimes ending in a real knockout. The fights are incredibly popular.

He speeds up the music and hustles the show along as the emcee shouts on the mic, presiding over a frenetic show of sex and colored lights and drinks and flying money. "It's all buzz," he says, proudly. "You can run a hovel, but if that hovel has a party that's known for some reason or another, they'll show up."

There's no VIP section in the bar. Everywhere is

ALL STAR STRIPPERS span the physical and ethnic spectrum, from tall and athletic to short and big-bottomed, from creamy hues to dark tones. But nearly all are the same in their belief that this job is temporary.

"I don't plan on doing this forever. This is a steppingstone," Kassidy says, a tall, lean nineteen-year-old. Lawrence shakes his head. All the girls say that, he says. A dancer at All Star, he recalls, gave an interview to a magazine once. "The quote was, 'I'm not like the rest of these girls. I'm not going to strip the rest of my life.' That magazine came out in 1999, and she had been here for five years. She still dances."

Every day, the girls have to deal with the jerks, the desperate and the weirdos, such as the old man who likes to spit in his hand and rub it all over the dancers' arms and stick his wet finger in their ears. Or the guy who likes sucking toes. Or the one who insists on smacking asses before he'll tip a dancer. Guys with strange fetishes who come here to say and do things they won't say or do at home. "You should see the nice doctor that we banned about six months ago," Lawrence says. "He liked to unveil himself under the

Dollar bills stacked on the bar, ready to make rain.

DJ booth, and he'd say, 'Touch Daddy's cock, child.' And he's a pediatrician."

As many as seventy dancers wander the floor here on a given day. Lawrence prods them to work out, to stay in shape, to save some money instead of blowing a night's earnings on shopping binges, to get out of the dressing room and onto the floor, fast. But he also tries to look out for them.

"The thing about entertainers is they're spoiled," he says. "A girl will make a grand in a night. You know what happens the next day? Three hundred dollars in hair and a trip to the mall. I tell them put that shit away because tomorrow night you might not make ten dollars. They don't listen."

The girls have backgrounds as varied as their looks.

Paris, twenty-five, says stripping is a family affair. "I seen my cousin coming home with a lot of money. I'm like, 'Wow,' so I started dancing." The cousin vanished for three years, strung out in Las Vegas. "My auntie finally got her back," she says, noting the aunt put her cousin into sex work in the first place. "They put her in rehab, she relapsed and got back on heroin. And now she has eight kids with seven different dads, and she's only thirty. The last I heard she was working at Wendy's." The aunt took in the kids, then died of a heart attack at forty-five. The ex-stripper got the kids back.

She wears an expression made blank by years of lap dances and stage work, the look of someone who has seen a *lot*. She claims she wants to quit stripping but can't. "Right now you can't find another job that's going to pay you every day like this," she says. She wants to be a nurse. Indeed, most of the girls here have a future career in mind, but no firm date when they'll start it.

Kassidy's on the other end, saying she plans on becoming a corporate attorney. But she's from the inner city, has the street argot to prove it and doesn't have much education. The odds are stacked.

Kassidy crawls across the stage.

Kassidy had her first strip club audition four months ago at a bar down the street from All Star. She got the gig on her innocent looks alone, even after admitting she couldn't dance. "He said I had a nice body, and said, 'You'll learn how to dance.'" Her unspoiled demeanor, the source of her popularity here, will soon be ruined, Lawrence says.

"That'll change in about four to six months," he says. "She'll lose that. Her innocence will be gone. She's potentially a super diva. And she'll be in this a while."

Kassidy and Paris are just two out of a hundred girls here with different stories that so far end the same—on a pole at a strip club on Eight Mile.

WHEN THE CLUB tore down its VIP wall, the idea was to chase out the hookers who stripped only to find johns. Lawrence thinks he's got the numbers down to about 20 percent of the girls, though he says with the VIP wall now down, they have to do it elsewhere if they want to do it at all. "It's going to happen," he says. "I discourage it as much as I can. It's not going to happen inside my building. They might go outside and try, though." If a stripper leaves for any reason, they're banned from returning for the night. "This is not Vegas," he says. "We do not do outcall here."

But other clubs do. He names dives around the city that are whorehouses, or clubs where girls can be bought and taken to a car or motel.

"A lot of girls don't think it's tricking," he says. "They just think, 'I know this guy; he knows I normally make $200 to $300 here, he's going to relieve me of that.' No, tricking is tricking. I'm old school—sell the sizzle, not the steak. Stop giving it away. You make more money just fulfilling the fantasy. I've seen girls who stand on stage and look around and they've fucked half the room. It's disgusting."

Inside his little office he's got a recently fired stripper's business card tacked to the wall, on which she had listed in-call and outcall prices. It's next to a handwritten "Most Unwanted" list on the wall of banned strippers. It runs into the dozens. Many are prostitutes.

He points to one stripper's stage name. "She's a nice girl, but she's banned from working here," he says. He fired her for tricking, then rehired her against his better sense. She went right back to it the first night. "I go in the men's restroom, I look under the stall, I see two pairs of shoes, twenty minutes later."

IT'S ANOTHER SATURDAY evening. Lawrence sits at a desk in his narrow office, getting ready to start the show all over again after a long grind the night before. "I fired five girls last night," he says, wearily. They were fighting with other strippers. Then they wanted to fight him after he threw them out. "I get one girl outside. In

The "Most Unwanted" list on the wall names strippers who've been banned from working at the club. Many are prostitutes.

Opposite: A dancer goes airborne while doing pole tricks.

one sentence she wanted to fistfight me, in the second sentence she said she's gonna come back and burn the bar down, in the third sentence she said I'll bet you I'll be working back at this bar next week."

It's an iron-fist policy. Small infractions that go unaddressed elsewhere get you fired here, because there's always someone out there who can take your place, someone younger or fresher, willing to follow the rules here. It's as strict at the club's entrance. A few nights before, a sixty-guy birthday party crashed a strip club down the street and took it over. "They were standing on the bar, pouring liquor on each other, paying for nothing," Lawrence says. "How you gonna stop them?" Situations like these are why the cameras and walkie-talkies and linebacker-size bouncers are in place. "In our mind, this is a compound," he says.

He and the other managers are wearing nice suits, part of the "corporate" tone they've worked to establish, part of the everyday battle to change the club's reputation. Every thug kept out, every prostitute thrown out, every joint snuffed out, is to them another black mark wiped off the club's image, another small attempt to prove that they can transform a once-sleazy strip club on Eight Mile, despite the history and the expectations against them.

But ultimately, despite all their efforts and the visible changes here, the truth may be that a strip club can rise only so high on the respectability meter, and Lawrence seems aware of that.

"This is a strip bar, therefore we are the scum of the earth," he says of the club's image with the police and neighbors. "But we're not. Other than forty-seven divas arguing, everybody's just having a good time."

Last Call

A Beautiful Old Bar with a Storied Past Hangs in Limbo

WEST JEFFERSON STARTS downtown and takes you to the middle of nowhere, from the city's skyscrapers into the wilderness of the Delray neighborhood, the closest thing to a ghost town within a city that, in some places, often resembles one.

Kovacs bar is one of a few places in Delray with the lights left on, an outpost for the handful of people who still work or live here, at Detroit's wild edges.

In every direction around it there's emptiness—barren fields, empty buildings, quiet streets. Crumbling little houses dot the blocks.

"The neighborhood? There isn't one," says Bob Evans, the bar's seventy-two-year-old owner. "Just a few neighborhood people on a street on this side and that side, but basically it's all vacant."

Bob and his wife Delores, sixty-four, bought the bar thirteen years ago, after she retired from Ford and he wound down a career in real estate. "It was a fling," he says of the purchase. Now it's a long-term relationship they want to end but can't.

They thought they'd retire once their bar was bought by the state to make room for a new bridge to Canada. But delays and a challenge by billionaire Manuel "Matty" Moroun, who insists on building another bridge next to his Ambassador Bridge a few miles up the river, have left the project—and the area—in limbo. All they can do is wait for the disputes and delays to be resolved.

"We can't put it up for sale," Bob says. "What are we going to tell the people—'Oh, we don't know when the bridge is coming through?' Who's going to deal with that unless you give it away? So we're stuck."

Kovacs owner Bob Evans waits for customers in his historic bar.

Their stunning bar, two stories of bricks and old wood, is 120 years old. Back then, Delray was an independent village growing through a steady inflow of Poles, Armenians and Hungarians. West Jefferson was still River Road, lined with tall maples and small businesses end to end. Dense housing sprang up to accommodate the immigrants.

The Solvay Process Co. opened a chemical plant here in 1894 and provided the village with jobs, paved streets, sewers and a horse-drawn, four-wheeled fire truck manned by company employees, who also built the neighborhood's first hospital. In 1901, Detroit Iron Works built two blast furnaces for iron making on nearby Zug Island, added to later by Great Lakes Steel Corp.

Detroit annexed the village in 1905. By then, companies were flocking here, drawn by the access to river transportation and natural resources. The small town gave way to factories and chemical plants.

As industry concentrated here, so did the pollution. The wildlife along the shore died off. River Road's trees stopped producing leaves in the spring. Powders from the factories would drizzle from the sky at night, leaving a thin film on houses and cars.

Residents who could afford to move away did so, starting a population exodus that continues today. By the 1950s, the I-75 freeway plowed through and took hundreds of houses, as did the construction of the wastewater treatment plant. Between that and the industries still in town, the air in Delray maintains a foul stench.

Only a few thousand people still live here, according to the 2010 census. Some would be relocated to make room for the second bridge to Canada, with a planned plaza to go right where Kovacs sits. But the project start date came and went while the dispute between Moroun and the state rages on. Now everyone just waits.

Bob pours himself a drink. He and his wife are their own customers tonight after a handful of steelworkers finished their drinks and headed home. An old-time neon sign glows in the window. There's baseball on TV.

Despite wanting to leave, Bob smiles with pride when he talks about the place. It was even in a movie once—*Hoffa*—back in the '80s. "There's a lot of history here," he says.

The building the bar is in was built in 1889. It began as the Angus Smith Hotel with a restaurant and beer garden selling cigars from a manufacturer on site. After Prohibition and a few name changes, a Hungarian named Micl Kovacs moved to Detroit from Ohio, bought it and turned it into a tavern. His son Steve took over when he returned from World War II and the old man died. "He marched all the way

The 120-year-old bar has undergone few changes since it opened.

through Europe in the infantry," Bob says. "He was a great big guy, a strong son of a bitch." Kovacs died in 1996, and his wife put his bar up for sale. Bob snapped it up.

"When I first bought it, sometimes I'd sit down at the end of the bar and just look at it—'Man, look at this place.'"

It's undergone few changes in its life. The walls are pine, the ceilings are high, the doors are thick and the mahogany Art Deco bar is massive. The walnut bar surface itself is made of a single piece of wood, reputed over the years to be the longest one-piece bar in the city. "I looked at it and said, 'God damn, this is one hell of a piece of tree,'" Bob says.

At first, he tended bar while Delores planned and cooked the lunches, which drew dozens of hungry steelworkers and truckers every day. "This would be filled in here and the overflow would have to go in the back," he says. "You ask anybody, this was a good lunch. We did spaghetti and meatballs, goulash, beef stroganoff. We always tried to keep the price down, keep it reasonable." In their time they've hosted retirement and Christmas parties, even a wedding reception.

But many of Delray's last holdout businesses were felled by the recession the past several years. U.S. Steel took over Zug Island, and after imposing layoffs a few years ago, the company prohibited the remaining contract workers from leaving for lunch, fearing they'd come back drunk and create liability issues. "They even got so bad they would send security around to check the cars at the bars, not only ours but from here to Wyandotte," Bob says.

Now the dining room sits empty, its tables and chairs neatly arranged but almost never used. "Losing the lunch trade was a big thing," Bob says. "That was 50 percent of our business."

They close the place before dark nowadays, mostly because the last steelworkers have left the area by then. Bob works days, Delores usually works evenings, though he'll stick around with her sometimes so she's not alone. "She gets the dock workers and city drivers, and some of the truck drivers; they pull in at night and they sleep in their trucks, so they park and come over here, have a few beers and go back, and they head out in the morning," he says.

They'll still sit and have drinks and talk with customers, and stay open later if someone is still thirsty or there's a good conversation going. But

There are signs everywhere that this bar was once surrounded by steel mills and factories.

DETROIT
IS A
UNION
TOWN

Evans waits for customers who would not be coming that tonight.

they're often alone, watching TV and waiting in case someone comes in for a few.

"It's so slow and it's so upsetting," Bob says. "I just go from day to day right now. It's a lot of stress. I would rather have somebody walk in and say, 'Hey, I'll give you this much money,' and I'll go out the door. But I want to keep them away from my wife 'cause she'll take a lot less. She's tired."

As with any fling, even one that's run its course, there's still some affection for the place, and they don't want to simply end things for good.

"You keep hanging on," Delores says. "You still pay your bills and you don't walk away. You just keep it going and you do what you have to do."

They finish their drinks. The sun is setting and the last customers are long gone. "You ready to go?" Bob says to her. She turns out the lights.

Land of the Lost

An Old-Time Diner Finds Itself the Center of Unwanted Attention

HELEN TURNER HAS a mean scowl on her face. Always. It's the look she gives customers at the diner where she works.

"I don't take no shit off of nobody," she spits in an Appalachian accent.

She's behind the counter at White Grove Restaurant, a tiny, genuinely retro diner on Second Avenue near Charlotte, in Detroit's skid row. Her customers are the city's underclass—addicts, prostitutes, the homeless and the insane. They spend their days aimlessly roaming their neighborhood here like zombies, slowly killing time and themselves, waiting for the next handout or the next quick score.

And nearly all of them come into the diner at some point, trying to pull a fast one.

"The attitude around here is, 'I don't have anything, so I'll try anything. What have I got to lose? I'll try any trick,'" says Linwood Martin, Turner's co-worker. "It's like they spend all of their time trying to conceive trickery. They're predators, vultures."

Martin and Turner have worked at the diner for decades, long enough to view everyone who walks in with suspicion. Both are in their late sixties and live nearby. Both have a dim view of the locals after their years among the crazies and the crooks.

"It's all mental cases around here," Turner says. "Ninety-nine percent mental cases. Might as well talk to that ceiling up there, you'd get more sense from it. And 95 percent of them are up to no good."

The diner opened in 1948. Its neighborhood, already rough back then, became the city's home of the homeless over time as the destitute flocked

Linwood Martin stands watch at the diner's door.

to the area, drawn by one another and the many social agencies that sprang up to service them.

"All them lunatics seemed to migrate down here," Martin says. "It had a big impact on us." The eatery's long-standing twenty-four-hour policy was trimmed back to closing before midnight a while ago because things became so unruly.

But there are swarms of them no matter the hour. They gather on curbs and corners, stumble around the middle of the road, lay down for naps in the grass or just stand around, like the ragged man in front of the diner wearing an old coat, staring inside with a face contorted by what can only be described as madness.

"When they bombed the trade center in New York with the planes, do you know that these people down here weren't aware of it?" Martin says with astonishment. "And if they were aware of it, it didn't shock them. You think you'd be shocked about a thing like that, being an American, being in the United States, right? Didn't faze them at all. I was amazed by that. Nobody talked about it. Nobody cared."

White Grove is a kitschy throwback, with six round stools at its narrow countertop, four at the front wall. An antique scale tells your weight and your fortune. The food is classic American diner fare: burgers, breakfasts, soups and fries, prepared by a cook in the back, out of sight. There's a large plate-glass window facing the street, covered in a metal grate. It gives a front-row seat to the show outside. They're always out there, in the snow and rain, in heat waves and cold spells, seemingly unaffected by their environment.

"They're so wrapped up in themselves, they don't notice anything around them except themselves and what they want," Martin says.

Most customers who wander into White Grove don't necessarily want food; free meals are brought into the area every day by social organizations, churches and volunteers. Instead, they usually ask for a handout or a cigarette, or they try to sell employees and customers something they've found or stolen.

"They're petty thieves," Martin says. "Really, they'll steal anything. They'll get it out of the garbage can." Sometimes they bring in anything shiny or metallic, figuring it must be worth something. "They come to me with this stuff, they don't even know what it is," he says.

If someone orders food, they'll usually pay in nickels and dimes, sometimes all pennies. A few will try to jump over the counter to snatch money from the cash register when it's open. Turner stops them cold. "I got somethin' for them," she insinuates, making a trigger-pulling gesture with her finger.

At White Grove in the Cass Corridor, Helen Turner's mean scowl wards off trouble.

The staff's aggressive demeanor keeps a lid on most trouble. Martin says he's been robbed at gunpoint only once, a surprising number, he says, considering the area. The gunman was a teen, maybe about sixteen years old. What the kid didn't know is Martin had a gun of his own and was weighing in his mind at that moment whether to pull it out and end the boy's life. "I could've killed him," he says. "But I said what the hell. He was just a kid. I told the lady here to give him the money."

Little human touches accent the diner and soften the tense atmosphere. A shelf behind the counter holds odd little figurines and quaint knickknacks—"dust collectors" as Turner calls them—that customers have given them over the years. Childlike depictions of meals hang on the wall below the block-lettered menu board, marker drawings on construction paper done by a woman who lives in the neighborhood. "She does all that fancy drawin' and writin' and stuff," Turner says.

As the cold afternoon rolls on, the customers come in waves, alone and in groups.

A haggard-looking, middle-aged woman walks through the door and asks for a light. She's given matches and staggers out, dazed.

A vagrant bounds in, eyes red and speech slurred, offering to sell for three dollars the free toiletries bag he just got from a church. But everyone around here has the same one. He gets no takers and leaves.

A trio of thugs drift to the stools, acting strange, scoping things out, until Martin snaps, "You gonna buy something or not?" They dither and leave reluctantly, but loiter outside. "They're waiting to see how much money you take out of your pockets," Martin says to a visitor.

A known dope dealer named Charles struts in, and Turner instantly recognizes him. He works the corridor of old Chinatown on Peterboro. He mumbles something to her.

"What's the problem, punk?" she barks back, facing him square. "You think you're a real pimp now 'cause you got that new truck, right?" Outside the window is a battered, used pickup he just drove up in. She threatens to shoot him. "I can kill you, and then you'll die," she says.

"I can take you wherever you want to go now," he replies with a stoned laugh, pointing to the truck.

"Go on down on the corner where you belong. You go down there and be the boss," she says sarcastically, staring him hard in the eye. He leaves.

Of a dozen people who come through, only one buys anything—a bowl of soup stretched out with fistfuls of crackers. He's a regular, a gentle old man.

Handmade signs announce the day's specials.

Visits from such customers allow Turner to let her guard down. Her face even softens while he's there.

But most of the time, nobody's eating and most everyone's scamming and Turner's had to be on guard all the time, ten hours a day, seven days a week, for a good part of thirty years. It's kept her on edge, ready to bark. Attack as defense. It's how you have to be here, in maybe the craziest neighborhood in town, where nearly everyone preys on everyone else but nobody's got anything worth taking.

"People are like damn fools around here," Turner says, lighting a cheap cigarette. She looks at the man who's still standing out front, looking inside the big window with those wide, crazy eyes, and she says, "You got to be observant at all times."

Street Fightin' Man

A Detroit Neighborhood Fights for Its Life, and an Ex-Cop Leads the Way

THE GUY WAS coming to shoot up Jack Rabbit's house in the middle of the night.

He'd already fired on other homes in the old east side neighborhood to scare residents he'd suspected of calling the cops on him.

It turned out the gunman was a drug dealer, and when neighbors had called the cops on him, or had gotten in his way, he retaliated by shooting up their houses.

Earlier that day, James "Jack Rabbit" Jackson—a retired Detroit cop—parked his car in front of the dealer's house and pointed a video camera at him in a blatant effort to disrupt his business. It drove the guy away for the day.

Now he was coming back for Jackson. And Jackson was waiting for him.

A car turned from Jefferson onto Chalmers. It drew closer, then slowed when it reached Jackson's house. The headlights panned the front of the home until they revealed the ex-cop sitting there on the otherwise dark porch, staring back.

He had a shotgun in his lap.

Jackson knows that, in Michigan, the law says that if your life's in danger, you have a right to use deadly force to defend yourself. That's why he keeps a baseball bat stashed on his porch. That's why he sat there late one night, waiting with that shotgun.

He had seen the old Chevy before and knew the drug-dealing gunman was inside it. The car belonged to a guy in the dealer's posse. But it didn't stay

Jack Rabbit holds a baseball bat as he watches for trouble from his front porch on Chalmers.

long. Between the armed ex-cop and the video camera mounted above the porch, the dealer had few options. The Chevy backed out of the driveway and left the same way it came.

Jackson is the de facto leader of the neighborhood, like an unofficial sheriff. He's sixty-three, burly and slower moving in his retirement. Everyone here knows him, and everyone here calls him Jack Rabbit, a nickname he has had for years. He's president of the Jefferson-Chalmers Homeowners Association, president of the Jefferson-Chalmers Citizens District Council and is on the Jefferson East Business Association's board of directors. He plows snow from the wintertime streets and sidewalks with his truck. He's the neighborhood lookout, and through his homeowners association, he offers a monthly reward for local crime tips. He's the one who urges everyone in his neighborhood to stay vigilant, the one who confronts criminals on the street and videotapes them.

"These guys are cowards," Jackson says. "They're not going to fight anyone that's going to go toe-to-toe with them."

The people who live here, like residents in dozens of similar Detroit neighborhoods with block clubs and associations, are battling to keep theirs from falling like so many others in the city. And guys like Jack Rabbit lead the charge.

THE JEFFERSON-CHALMERS NEIGHBORHOOD lies by the Detroit River, on several long streets south of the intersection it's named after. Its 1920s-era shopping district is on the National Register of Historic Places. Its eclectic bungalows and Arts and Crafts houses, built early last century, still have beauty and character despite weathering over the years. Vacant lots have appeared on side streets, and some foreclosed houses have boards on their windows, but most blocks are still dense with owner-occupied homes where lawns are kept mowed and the houses are kept up.

"It's a great neighborhood. Lots of good people live around here, been around here for years," Jackson says. "Where else can you get this close to the water? Just five blocks down the road it costs half a million, three-quarters of a million to live," he says, pointing toward Grosse Pointe. By contrast, many homes on this side of Alter Road, the border of Detroit, sell for less than $10,000 nowadays.

But there's a war going on here. On one side are longtime residents trying to maintain a safe, desirable neighborhood. On the other side is their enemy:

the drug dealers, the burglars, the petty thieves, the lifelong criminals who prey on the regular folks here. Some invade from bordering neighborhoods; a few live right within it. Though they've always been a problem, there appears to be more of them since the economy tanked.

It's a war of little battles. The residents fight by lighting their yards, videotaping drug deals, harassing scrappers and chasing off thieves.

Their enemy attacks in shocking ways. Like taking over the homes of bedridden old people. Like recruiting kids as dope-house spotters and runners. Like killing people's dogs.

"There's one old lady, she lives on Manistique, and she's had problems where the guys have come and poisoned the dogs so they wouldn't be able to bark when they heard them coming to break in," Jackson says. "They poisoned several of them down there. She said they've killed dogs up and down her street."

The same thing happened to B.J. Lewis, a thirty-year resident of Ashland Street. She once had two German shepherds for protection. "Several years ago I went to open up my kitchen door and there's a guy in my yard, and you know what he told me? 'What are you gonna do, bitch?'" remembers the seventy-one-year-old. "I just opened the door and let the dogs out and I called 911." The dogs chased him off. "What would have happened to me if I didn't have the dogs?"

She didn't have them much longer. Someone came and killed them. The usual method around here is lacing hot dogs or chicken with antifreeze. The dogs like its sweet taste. They die pretty quickly after eating it.

"We seem to be under siege," Lewis says. She's got one dog left, a pet she won't let out in the yard alone anymore. "My dog is about the only dog that's living at this end of the street. There used to be dogs on both sides, all the way down. These criminals are terrorists."

IN THIS WAR, the enemy infiltrates neighborhoods and ruins them from within. Jackson recounts the ways.

Some move into an elderly relative's home and take it over, selling drugs in the living room as the homeowner lies helpless in bed, he says. "She's not aware of what's going on, she's got some young people there running the house, maybe her kids, she's upstairs in her bed, can't get out of the bed, those kids let somebody come in there, make a little money."

Some buy silence or space from a stranger. "They'll pay a little something to use the house and they kind of blend in with the family that lives in the home," he says. "They're only getting Social Security or SSI or whatever it is, and the guy wants to sell drugs out of there. A little bit of money ensures that adults won't call the police on them."

Some hire middle school kids as drug couriers, training them for lives of crime. "These guys have literally taken over these neighborhoods, and they're the only ones hiring in the neighborhood," Jackson says. "They'll hire your kids to run back and forth between the house and the cars. They give them commission."

Some hoist the smaller kids into the milk chutes still in the walls of the old homes here, where they climb into the house, steal what they can and pass things outside through the narrow opening.

Some steal the infrastructure, the very skeleton of the neighborhood. "It was a Saturday, and Jack called me in the morning, said he's following two guys with a fire hydrant over here, heading to the junkyard," says fifty-five-year-old Keith Hines, Jackson's neighbor and partner in crime fighting. "These two drug addicts had taken that hydrant and put it in their car." He and Jackson accosted the scrappers at the junkyard, had the yard owner block their car from leaving, even interrogated them on video until police arrived. Next to their car was a pile of street signs someone else had sawed off and brought in.

"It's a constant battle," Hines says. He bought a three-story house on Chalmers thirteen years ago. "We don't have it as bad as a lot of other people do, but it's a constant battle."

Things like these, small compared to more violent crimes, are nonetheless what slowly bring down a neighborhood, driving people to move away, launching a cycle of abandonment and blight. That's why, residents here say, it's important to confront the criminals every time, to stop the cancer before it spreads.

"This stuff goes unnoticed by the average person," Jackson says. "We're fighting. That's literally what it is. We're fighting to save our neighborhood."

A NEW WENDY'S restaurant might not mean much in other neighborhoods. But out here it's an important symbol, helpful in attracting other businesses.

"Wendy's has come down here before and they left," Jackson says. He's convinced all the break-ins and robberies they suffered drove them out. "They

James "Jack Rabbit" Jackson (left) with neighbor Keith Hines.

were only here a while, so we wanted to make sure they didn't leave us again."
So when the burglaries started, Jackson and Hines hid one night in the bushes
bordering the restaurant, armed with their video cameras, waiting for the
suspects to come back. After a couple long, dark nights lying there in the dirt,
they saw them return.

"Nobody could seem to get them," Jackson says. "But in just a couple days
we got them, at about two, three o'clock in the morning." They gave the
tapes to the police, who used them to find and arrest them.

Jackson is Wendy's biggest booster. He eats there often, takes breaks
from his towing work there, holds some neighborhood meetings there. "It's
important to support them, to spend money at local businesses like this,"
he says.

Since retiring from the police department's gang squad a decade ago,
Jackson has operated a towing and snow plowing business. He's often seen
patrolling his neighborhood's streets in his tow truck, crawling along at near
idling speed, peering into yards, looking around corners, seeing what's what.
He knows who lives where, who's on vacation, who's a stranger. He waves to
just about everyone he sees. They all know him and wave back. His habits are
those of an old policeman.

Jackson takes pride in the neighborhood, and he'll take you on a tour to
point out little successes, like new housing that's rising across Jefferson, the
corner liquor store that burned down but was rebuilt even bigger and the old
houses that have new siding or a fresh coat of paint. They're welcome signs
of life, of continuity.

"This lets you know the city's not dead," he insists. "It's alive, man. It's alive."

A DIRTY, HAGGARD little man named Roy walks into Wendy's and sits just two
tables over from Jackson.

His wool hat has holes and his beard is tangled and bushy. He orders nothing.
He just sits and loiters. Jackson knows him well: "He's one of our bad guys.
He's got strict orders not to come on Chalmers."

Roy is a lifelong criminal, Jackson says, one of several around here who
plague the neighborhood.

A few months back, Roy and a crackhead in a wheelchair pushed a lawnmower
past Jackson's house. From experience, he knew right away it was stolen,
probably from the shed of the crackhead's own elderly mother, he figured.
Jackson phoned her family.

"I said, 'Does Mrs. Hall's son have permission to let somebody take a lawnmower from her house?' and the guy says, 'Hell no. She doesn't even want him over there. They stole it if they got it.'"

So Jackson and a neighbor caught up with the two men down the street. They grabbed Roy and started shoving him around, grilling him about the stolen mower. "It was funny as hell, because once we grabbed Roy and collared him, jacked him up a little bit, the guy in the wheelchair's like, 'You're on your own!' to Roy. And Mrs. Hall was in the house, didn't even know the lawnmower was stolen."

Another time, they caught Roy trying to break into someone's house while the homeowner was away. "He comes up out of the driveway all big-eyed and everything. You know you got him. I said, 'What are you doing?'" Roy stammered. Jackson punched him in the face. Roy pleaded innocence. But a prybar poked out of his waistband.

"So we jacked his ass up right out there in the street," Jackson says. "People are laughing and shit—'Go! Beat the shit out of that guy!'"

Yet Roy sat inside Wendy's, unconcerned, just feet away from the man who's the bane of his criminal existence.

"He knows he's all right as long as he's not on Chalmers," Jackson explains. "He knows he's gonna get his ass whipped on Chalmers. I'm harmless anywhere else, but if I catch him on Chalmers, or anywhere breaking in, that's it."

Their cat-and-mouse game would be amusing if guys like Roy didn't make life so miserable for people here, didn't give them another reason to give up on the neighborhood.

"POLICE RESPONSE IS abominable," says seventy-eight-year-old Ann Johnson. Someone tried to shoot up her neighbor's house one night, she says. But they were apparently inexperienced at holding an automatic weapon and it fired wildly, spraying her house too. She found eight bullet holes inside. "I was in bed, and a bullet went though my pillow, about four inches from my head. If I had been lying on my left side I wouldn't be here today." It took three visits, she says, to get police to take a report.

Many residents say they don't bother calling 911 anymore because police response is slow for all but the most serious crimes. It's as if they're on their own out here. "We feel like old pioneers sometimes," Johnson says.

Budget cuts over the years and the move from thirteen city police precincts to six consolidated "districts" five years ago made things worse, residents say, a failure the police have acknowledged and now plan to reverse. "When they closed the precinct down over here, right away there was a difference," Hines says. "Now, if someone is breaking into your house and you call the police maybe they'll show up today, but there's a 75 to 80 percent chance they won't. If you're lucky, they might show up. And the bad guys know it. The criminals can pretty much do what they want."

A burglar was rampaging one day on Ashland, going from house to house, trying to get inside, Lewis says. "Three of us called 911 all day long, 'cause this guy took his time, he knocked on doors, jumped over fences. We called 911, they never showed up. You always think to call 911, but it doesn't always work out."

Police spokesman John Roach, second deputy chief of DPD, doesn't offer excuses. "We make no bones that response time in some categories of our runs is not where anybody wants it to be right now," Roach says. "The chief has said that openly."

"We have to look at ourselves as the emergency room triage from time to time," he continues. "We'd like to treat sprained ankles when they happen, but if there's a gunshot wound, for example, then we have to take care of that first. Things like a breaking and entering, after the fact, where a suspect is long gone, those typically take us longer to get to. But it's because we're dealing with something more immediate at the time."

The city has neighborhood crime statistics online, but even Roach admits they're not entirely accurate because so many people don't file police reports. So the citywide figures of 17,428 violent crimes and 53,095 property crimes—numbers for 2008, the latest year with available FBI stats—most likely fall short of the true mark.

"The most important thing is making sure crimes get reported. People have stopped reporting a lot of property crimes because there has been a conditioned response that DPD isn't going to respond anyway. It makes everyone's job a little harder. But you can understand why people feel that way because it's something born out of past experience."

Residents such as Jackson and Hines blame a lack of police presence and slow response time for the prevalence of nuisance crimes in the area, but most don't fault the officers themselves.

"I can't blame it on the police," Hines says. "They're shorthanded now. They're going from one call to another. The old days of them sitting in a restaurant with a doughnut and a coffee are gone. But those days were when they were able to keep crime under control."

TIGH CROFF'S HOME on Manistique was broken into three times in one week just before the holidays. Then he came home three days after Christmas and found two men in his backyard in what looked to be the fourth burglary. That's when he lost it.

Police say a furious Croff chased one of the unarmed men out of the yard and down the street about a block before the suspect got winded and stopped running. Croff is accused of then shooting him in the chest, killing him right there on the street. He was charged with second-degree murder but was sentenced to two years in prison on a reduced charge.

It happened just outside Jackson's neighborhood, but it was close enough, and familiar enough, for him to understand Croff's anger. "We want to support that guy as much as we can," Jackson says. "Everybody in Detroit should support him. You go out in the neighborhood, talk to the neighbors, they say he takes care of the neighborhood."

The same is said about Alvin Davis. During Memorial Day weekend last year, after someone broke into his elderly mother's house on Marlborough, a couple streets over from Jackson, Davis, a federal agent with the Department of Homeland Security, spent the weekend allegedly combing the neighborhood, interrogating several residents, even forcing one into his car at gunpoint. He's now serving four years in prison for unlawful imprisonment and assault.

The state law says deadly force is acceptable as self-defense, only if your life is threatened. The law doesn't say you can shoot an unarmed man who's running away or chase down neighbors and hold them for interrogation sessions. The law sets a fairly clear line between self-defense and vigilantism.

Despite their actions, Croff and Davis are heroes in the Jefferson-Chalmers area. "When they broke in her house, he lost it," Lewis says. "Can you imagine someone breaking into your house three times in a week and you have to go to work and wonder what's going on at your house? It's been a battle. So we empathize with Mr. Croff and Mr. Davis, and a lot of us are going to show up, if this man goes to court to support him."

Police spokesman Roach has heard the neighbors justify such alleged actions by citing slow police response, but he says that, of the three times Croff says his property was burglarized, he reported only one incident. "We had a B&E that was discovered on the nineteenth of December" on Croff's property, he notes. "That's the only one we got a call on. So there were others that were not brought to our attention. And it was dispatched two minutes after the call came in."

He acknowledges, though, that sometimes, when faced with a situation in which they feel preyed on over and over, some people will react violently. "I don't know if there's anything short of catching every suspect that would prevent somebody from taking drastic steps," he says.

One thing the neighbors note, though, is that Davis's alleged rampage had an effect. "When he did that, all the crime around here dropped down to zero for a while," Hines says.

LEWIS STANDS ON her porch with her shaggy dog, Bossman, and offers reasons why she stays here: her good neighbors, their urban garden in the summer, how her dog waits out front for the schoolchildren to pass by every day, the diversity of people on her street.

She's got a nice arrangement of gardens behind her house, which she puts a lot of effort into. But they're penned in by two fences, one erected within the other, with a zone in between, to make it harder for someone to hop into her yard.

It reflects how life is in many Detroit neighborhoods—people hope for the best but brace for the worst.

Then an unkempt man wanders up and stands in front of Lewis's house, in the cold. "Do you have anything I can have? Anything?" he asks. "No, love," she replies softly. She doesn't know him, she says; he just wandered onto her street. "He's a troubled soul." Normally the elderly woman will give street people her recyclable bottles, but she's got none right now. He remains standing there, staring, as she steps inside.

The episode is a metaphor for what's happening here, where residents in a once-grand neighborhood find their streets raided by addicts and criminals who destroy the quality of life for those living here.

B.J. Lewis stands on her porch with her dog, Bossman.

"The neighborhood's changed drastically around us," Jackson says. "Yet you look at Chalmers, we've had our share of lost houses, but it's still pretty good."

Go a few streets in either direction though, and the vacant lots and burned-out houses grow in number. It's from out there, beyond the still-nice neighborhood's borders, that the criminals are invading Jefferson-Chalmers.

And when they show up here, Jack Rabbit's waiting.

"If we're gonna move this city forward, man, the guys that live in the neighborhoods are gonna have to circle the wagons and do what we can, you know what I'm saying? You do what you gotta do to keep the neighborhood afloat. We've got to keep this city afloat."

The Storyteller

A Teacher without Students Living in a Museum without Visitors

HER GRANDFATHER WAS a slave.

So was her grandmother, who had white features she inherited from the man who'd raped her mother.

When Bettie Birch was growing up in Jim Crow Mississippi, these were the kinds of stories the family would tell the children. For her, as it was for many others, black history wasn't exactly history; it was memories of the recent past and the experiences of the present.

"They passed the stories down to us," she says. "We would always get together as family and pass down oral information, which was not always written down. They always told us, 'Don't forget.' It was just the way you were reared. It was part of the culture. You were living in it."

That storytelling tradition left such an impression on her that she devoted her life to teaching black history to others, first as a Detroit Public Schools teacher, then on a local cable access TV channel and finally from inside her northwest Detroit home, which she has transformed into what she calls the Ant T Bettie OK Puppets Museum.

Her rooms have become galleries. Some are filled with colorful paintings; others have shelves holding dozens of figurines and statues. Just about every object has meaning, a story behind it.

A display is devoted to a makeshift pictorial family tree, with photos arranged in descending chronology. At the very top are the oldest, most faded ones. She's drawn likenesses of the people there are no photos of and put them in their place to fill the gap.

The puppets that the museum is named after are gathered in the basement. The biggest ones are life size, as tall and wide as people. They stand upright, their heads nearly brushing against the ceiling. Smaller puppets recline on a couch. More are packed away, out of sight.

Presiding over them is a big red papier-mâché ant, referred to in the pun in the museum's name. Ants cooperate with each other and work together, Birch likes to say. People should do likewise, she would tell children. She used to dress up as an ant when saying it to them.

Now that she's retired, she doesn't get to dress up in those costumes anymore. She won't hold events at her house for fear of bothering the neighbors with a lot of traffic and commotion. And the TV shows ended long ago. She's a performer in search of a stage, a teacher looking for a class, living in a museum without visitors.

"I wanted to set up in a huge building and just arrange puppet and tutorial programs, but these building people want too much money, and I don't have money," she says. All those empty storefronts around town, she points out, and they have the nerve to charge that much for rent? "That shows how they are draining Detroiters," she sneers.

So for now, the museum is in her house, its objects accenting some rooms and taking over others. Everything in it has some personal connection to her life, like the unfinished dollhouse model of the house she grew up in, or the painting of the family land showing the tree her father hinted was used for lynchings.

Don't ever cut that tree down, he told the family.

For Birch, the personal illustrates the historical and often parallels it. "It's the history of America," she says. "We can't change it, so we may as well tell the truth."

She grew up just after the Depression in a Mississippi country town called Scooba, little more than a patch of fields given a name. Her father bought a part of the land his own father worked as a slave, moved into a former slave shack by the road and added onto it. That was her home growing up. It was better than the alternative, she says.

"Being a child of parents who were slaves, he said his children would never live in a white man's house," she says. After the Civil War, most freed slaves found themselves with no money, property or education and nowhere to go, and many wound up working as sharecroppers for the same plantation owners they were once owned by. "My father was smart enough not to make his children grow up in that," she says. "So before he got married, he bought the land and built the house."

The parents later moved their eight children to nearby Meridian, the closest big town, so they could get an education. The first thing they learned was how to get by under segregation. "I lived in the South during that time," she says. "Now, kids think it's strange. They're not used to it. For me to tell them that, they just sit there. They don't believe it."

She has stories of little gestures of protest, like when they were kids and would move too slow to the back of the bus when told to or taking the sign indicating seats for blacks and moving it to the seats for whites when nobody was looking. Little things, but they're important to her.

She fled north to Detroit, attended Wayne State University and went to work for the Detroit Job Corps, where she ran into so many high school dropouts she felt compelled to become a schoolteacher. She spent twenty-five years teaching black history, art and English composition in several city schools.

That's when she started creating the puppets and putting on the shows. "My stories are real-life stories of black people, like for instance, Frederick Douglass, Benjamin Banneker," she says. "Small black kids, you didn't see nothing in the magazines but white people, or you didn't see them on TV. Well, you wonder, did they ever do anything? If your parents don't look like that, did they ever do anything? That's one of the reasons I did it."

She did a few shows on Barden Cablevision public access in the early '90s. Her basement was the studio. "I had like a little theater in my laundry room and they would tape it here, and then I would go to the TV station and they would put it together and put it on TV," she says. The episodes had names like "Who Discovered Peanut Butter?"

But the TV shows ended, her teaching career wound down and her house became a museum. "I had so much piled up at school and I didn't want to leave all my material there, so some I threw away, some I gave away and some I hauled back here."

Her days now are spent tending to the lush plants that crowd her windows, writing books of poetry and making paintings. She loves retirement, she insists.

But gnawing at her comfort is the sense that kids nowadays don't understand their legacy, she says. Or the debt they owe. "So many children don't know who they are, they don't know a thing about slavery," she says. "I feel that up here some people haven't taken advantage of their opportunities. Some people have been able to go to school all their life. Some people have been able to get jobs. But they don't. They don't aspire to do nothing but buy clothes or party or get a car. To me it's just a waste of energy, and I'm wondering is it because they don't know? It just burns me up."

Bettie Birch at home with her life-size historical puppets.

That frustration makes her want to get back out and pass along the old stories again, if only part time. "I've decided I'm gonna go out and do some storytelling," she says. Even though she's given up on finding a building to rent, she's trying to find somewhere to perform. Maybe at schools, or a library. Anywhere someone will sponsor a former teacher and her historical performances. "But I can't take all the puppets out. I'll just take maybe one or two of them, for the children."

Now she just needs a place to take them.

Rollin' in Dough

A Family's Neighborhood Business Is Rich in Sugary Tradition

YOU CAN SMELL the doughnuts half a block away. The strong, sugary scent drifts out from Dutch Girl Donuts on Woodward near Seven Mile, twenty-four hours a day, into the neighborhood around it.

It's perfumed the air that way for sixty-three years, wafting past houses where the shop's customers once lived before moving away, past the empty spots where houses once stood when the shop opened.

Over the years, nearly all of its neighboring stores left the city one by one, including next door's Sydney Bogg candy shop, after holding out longer than most around it. Between the doughnuts and the candy, the air on the block was infused with a sweet aroma for years.

"I really miss Sydney Bogg," says Jon Timmer, twenty-nine, the grandson of Dutch Girl's founder, as he rolls dough for another batch. Outside his big window, the candy store's fading, hand-painted wall sign faces back at him. "I think it's in Berkley now. It's still the same candy, still the same family and all that, but they just wandered away from the area."

But the doughnut shop stayed behind, through the population flight, through the crumbling of the neighborhood, even after robberies shook up the staff.

"We've been here a long time," he says. "My grandparents moved to Detroit because they knew it would be a big city, there'd be people that would want that, they'd get that followship, people that come in and enjoy what we do. Our customers would have to travel farther if we moved."

But the family has been tempted, he admits, to follow the exodus to the suburbs.

"I mean, we've probably all thought that a little bit, whether to move," he says. "But we've never really had that discussion because the doughnut shop's always been a Detroit thing."

Jon comes in at 5:00 a.m. nearly every day to make hundreds of doughnuts in the wall of windows at the store's front, where he's on display as he works, lit like a movie screen in the early morning darkness. He spreads dough on the wood table his grandfather hand-carved a lifetime ago. Sometimes there's a line of customers waiting for the first batch to come out of the fryer, soft and warm, before the sun's even up.

THERE ACTUALLY IS a Dutch girl for whom the shop was named.

She's Jon's now-eighty-eight-year-old grandma, Cecelia, who lives in a northern suburb and needs a walker to get around these days, so she rarely makes it down to the shop. But she still runs things from home, doing the payroll and paperwork and handling the scheduling.

She and her husband, John Timmer, used to live in the State Fair neighborhood, just blocks from the doughnut bakery. "It was a beautiful neighborhood. All lovely homes. The houses were all well kept," she says, using the same words so many other former Detroiters use about their old neighborhoods. Hers is a blighted mess now.

After returning home from World War II, in 1946 John moved the family from Grand Rapids, where they had a small doughnut shop, to open a bigger place in Detroit.

"They looked at Lansing and said it's too small," says Cecelia's son Gene Timmer, sixty-three. "They said, 'Let's go for Detroit. Let's go for a big city.' At the time there were maybe only a half a dozen doughnut shops in the area. If you could make doughnuts you could really do well."

They had no idea.

"He said, 'The first night after we take in $100 I'll take you out to dinner,'" Cecelia remembers, "and I said, 'Well, that will be one sweet date!' Just the second day we were open we took in $100." This was back when they had to earn it forty cents at a time, the cost of a dozen doughnuts then.

John died in 1966. Gene, barely out of his teens, had to take over. He still comes in every evening at 10:00 p.m. and works half the night. Some regulars know his schedule and give him grief when he's late, Jon says. "If he's watching a baseball game he comes in a little late and they know it, they're like, 'Where are my doughnuts? Were you watching baseball?'"

The shop looks about the same as it did in the early '50s. The few changes include the addition of a dough-shaping tool to spare the fingers of those who for years made the doughnuts by hand and the bulletproof glass that Gene added after a robbery years ago.

"I hated to do it," he says, "but pretty soon you like it for the safety factor. We had spikes up there too, and a guy still jumped over it, little agile guy. I was here and we gave him the money and he jumped right back over." After that they extended it closer to the ceiling.

But on most days the little window by the cash register is open anyway, to keep the face-to-face interactions going. "It's a lot of fun down here interacting with the customers, and having those people that come in—'Hey, how you doing?' We talk to them in the morning," Jon says. "It's nice."

WHEN HE WAS younger, Jon didn't really want to be part of the family business but sometimes worked at the shop while in high school. He joined the U.S. Navy after graduation to see the world. He got more than he bargained for— 9/11 happened and he was sent to Afghanistan, Iraq and North Korea. "You get stationed on a ship and then all of a sudden all that stuff happens. You don't really know that's what you're signing up for."

Once home, he went to work at the shop and gained an appreciation for it. "At that point, I wasn't really ready to work here," he says. "I wanted something else. But now the family, I get the reason why Dad's been here so long and why they started it."

Jon prides himself on treating his job as a craft, taking time with each batch. "Business has really picked up because he makes them better," Gene says. "He's really concentrating on making a good doughnut. You think you're good right away and you can learn it in a little while, but then to really get it to where everything is looking really good all the time, that's a real trick."

He and his dad make most of each day's doughnuts. Each specializes in different kinds—Jon makes rising doughnuts, the airy kind; Gene makes thick, cake ones. They make a couple dozen flavors between them.

They're a close family, living and working together, even creating batches of homemade Dutch Girl silkscreen T-shirts in their basement. "We don't

The Timmer family inside Dutch Girl Donuts. They've sold doughnuts in Detroit for over six decades.

Above, left: The line at Dutch Girl Donuts forms early in the mornings.

have to have a shop meeting really, 'cause we can just have dinner," Jon says. "The downside is dinner is usually doughnut-related. Not food-wise, but conversation; they'll be talking about the doughnut shop."

Just about everything at Dutch Girl is old-fashioned, a continuation of a tradition, like the original recipes they use, like passing the business from father to son to grandson, like staying behind in a city that most people fled. Even the wall-size windows are a throwback in a town full of stores with glass block and iron bars where unprotected windows used to be.

Maintaining and carrying on that history means something to this family. "This whole place, my dad used to stand there," Gene says, pointing to the table where the doughnuts are formed in front of the big window, where his son leans over, making another batch. "And I stand in the same spot. I think that's really neat."

Brothers in Arms

Detroit's Last Gun Shop Barrels On

"DOES ANYBODY HERE have a problem with taking a life?" asks sixty-nine-year-old General Laney, owner of Laney's Guns and Supplies on Detroit's east side. "If you're not capable of taking a life then you're not in the right place," he warns, "'cause you might have to take a life. You have no choice because the person who wants to take your life has no feeling for you."

Laney should know—he was once shot six times.

He's teaching a self-defense and concealed weapons permit class at his store. The students sitting before him here look uneasy at times.

Aside from an old house, his store's the lone building on the block. It's along a terrible stretch of Chene that was once part of Poletown but now's in an urban prairie. Surprisingly, in a town full of guns, Laney's is the only place left where you can buy them legally within city limits.

Laney's sells firearms and ammunition, hosts the aforementioned classes and has a shooting range in the basement for which you can rent guns. From the 1920s until he bought it in the 1990's, the building housed a billiards room—it was a place to shoot both pool and guns.

The main floor is cluttered with stacks of files, piles of newspapers and buckets of bullets. A space heater crackles, glows orange in the otherwise cold room. Two Dobermans—Sarge and T-Man—are locked in the back. Laney sits at a front desk, surrounded by stacks of paperwork and shelves stocked with ammo.

"This neighborhood was originally a white neighborhood, and it had the gun range," says Laney, who is black. "When black people moved in, it was still there but it wasn't made available to black people. Things changed when I got here."

Laney grew up in Inkster, where his family's pawnshop sold a few guns now and then. "Inkster's a little different than Detroit when it come to guns," he says. "Different way of thinking. My family's from the South anyway, and our thinking about guns is a little different than in Detroit."

His core belief, one that he's spent his life espousing, is that gun laws target blacks. "Gun control in Detroit is racist to begin with. You heard of Dr. Sweet?" he asks, referring to the case of Ossian Sweet, a black physician who, with his family, was tried and eventually acquitted for shooting into a white mob that attacked their home when they moved into an all-white neighborhood in 1925.

Soon after, the state passed stringent gun-control laws, known as Public Act 372 of 1927. Laney sees those laws aimed squarely at blacks, a reaction to the verdict. "After the Sweet case, the Michigan legislature said we couldn't allow black people to have guns, and that's how Michigan gun laws come about. Gun control is race control. It has been that way to keep blacks in servitude." Another hero of his is Robert F. Williams, a 1960s advocate of armed self-defense for the black community and an inspiration to the Black Panthers.

Laney has become nationally notorious in the gun industry for his views, eventually drawing the law's attention. In 1999, six years after he bought the place, the Wayne County Sheriff's Office sent an undercover cop into the store to make a "straw" purchase, in which a qualified buyer purchases a weapon on behalf of someone who can't legally buy it—in this case, it was another cop posing as a minor. The sting resulted in charges against Laney and two other gun shops. Laney fought the case all the way to the Michigan Supreme Court and was exonerated. He says he spent $50,000 on legal bills defending himself.

"They tried to set me up," he claims. "It's a moral victory." A gun group gave him a trophy consisting of two brass balls to commemorate his tenacity. "It's a thing that should never have come to court anyway. When court was over I said, 'Your honor, when you're dead and in your grave, when you feel that water coming in, it will not be rain. That will be me pissing on you.'"

His partner in crime prevention is seventy-year-old Walter Martin. He teaches gun safety down in the basement's roughshod gun range, where puddles of water pool on its cement floor, dripping from the leaky roof on rainy days.

General Laney inside the city's last gun shop.

Sheets of metal are positioned to direct wayward bullets into a muffling pile of old boards. A beam of wood holds a series of paper targets in place.

"From back here I've been hit with some of these," Martin says, standing at the shooting line, reminiscing about ricocheting bullets. He unconsciously shields his groin with his hand as he talks. "A woman was shooting, and I got hit right on the head of my dick!" he suddenly shares. "But it didn't hurt. It just come and fell. So about two, three months later a lady's down here shooting, the damn bullet ricocheted, hit my damn dick. I said 'What the hell's going on here!'"

Neither man tolerates thug behavior or incorrect shooting techniques like pointing the gun sideways, gangsta-style. "We don't play that," Martin says. "You come down here and shoot right or you get the hell out. In the classes we promote safety. I don't give a damn if people never hit the target. You're learning how to handle the weapon safely." They once taught a blind man how to shoot toward the sound of an intruder.

Every few minutes a new customer steps in—each with a story. A mumbling guy brings in a broken handgun, saying he's moving down South and doesn't want to leave his elderly mother alone, unprotected. He needs the weapon fixed. A short, woeful woman says she needs a gun permit because she works the closing shift at a liquor store and is scared for her life.

"We've had women come down here, old ladies come down, seventy-something years old," Martin says. "Like I tell people, when you need the police, he's not never there." The common thread among customers here is fear of random violence.

"I've been carjacked a few times," says Tawon Baldwin, twenty-five, as he sits in Laney's CCW class early one morning. "And I felt like I didn't want to ride around with no illegal gun, get charged with it." He wants to be legit.

"I've been carjacked too. Twice," says twenty-eight-year-old Selicia Huff, the only other applicant here. "I stay in a pretty bad neighborhood, so not only do I want it for protection; I figured if I have one I should know the correct use."

Laney can sympathize—he was a landlord once, and an angry renter once unloaded a gun on him, leaving six bullet holes in his body. "You'll never forget it when it happens," he says. "I have flashbacks of him shooting at me."

The classes here go beyond firearm safety to include chilling inner-city survival tips. "Don't let nobody get you down on your knees begging for your life," Laney warns the students. "If you fight you could win. And for God's sake, don't let nobody put you in the trunk of no car. You definitely not going to win there."

Walter Martin shoots inside the gun shop's basement firing range.

Everything at Laney's is designed to prepare those who figure they might one day stare down the barrel of a gun. In Detroit, those odds aren't so remote in some places.

"Somebody else is going to determine when this is going to happen, so you have to be prepared for what it is," Laney tells them. "You can't say who or where or when it's going to happen. If it does happen, one thing about it—you must win."

Soldiering On

A Real Horseman Keeps History Alive
and Brings Some Country to the City

HIS OFFICE SMELLS like horse manure. But James Buchanan doesn't mind at all.

He's standing behind his small desk on a sweltering July afternoon, putting on a heavy wool uniform worn by soldiers long ago.

Buchanan is in charge here at the Buffalo Soldiers Heritage Center, which lies at the edge of Rouge Park, on the city's western border.

The stink comes from the horses down the hall, in stables that are separated from his office by only a little door. This place belonged to the Detroit Mounted Police until the storied unit was shut down for a while five years ago and this spot was closed for good.

The cops left behind an ancient red brick building, some old wood stables and an abandoned plot of land where Buchanan and a few friends would bring their horses and ride around.

"And every time, before we'd even get the horses off the trailer, kids would come by to see them," Buchanan says.

So he hatched an idea, contacted city officials and was given permission to put horses back in the barn, corral the yard with a white picket fence and give city kids a rare chance to see and ride horses and ponies.

As he pulls on the layers of his uniform in the July heat, families sit outside on a picnic table in the shade of an overhanging tree, waiting for a ride on an animal many out here have never seen in person.

James Buchanan with his horse at his west side corral.

And when he steps outside, Buchanan hopes that maybe one of them will notice the old uniform, or see the small displays just outside his office, the ones with faded photos of black soldiers long ago, and ask him to explain the story behind them, to find out what inspires a man to dress in a thick wool costume on a hot summer day.

Years ago, Buchanan was riding horses in Canada, the closest place someone from Detroit could do that back then, when a fellow rider told him about the Buffalo Soldiers.

"When I was in school, I knew about Billy the Kid, Jesse James, the Dalton boys, but I never heard of someone by the name of Ben Hodges, who was a famous cowboy, and I didn't know about the Rufus Buck Gang, who were outlaws, but over the years of studying about these young, courageous men, I found out there were other ethnicities out there that you don't have in our history books. So then I was captured by it."

THE NAME BUFFALO Soldiers originally referred to the four all-black army units formed in 1866, staffed with former slaves and soldiers who'd fought in the Civil War. Their name was reportedly given to them by the Cheyenne tribes they were sent out West to fight and referred either to the troops' fierce fighting style or their curly hair, which the native fighters, it was said, thought resembled that of a buffalo. Either way, the troops took the name as a compliment.

Buchanan studied their history, found friends and fellow riders who shared his fascination and formed a local chapter under the national Buffalo Soldiers Cavalry Association dedicated to preserving the memory of the forgotten troops.

They slowly assembled expensive replica uniforms, the old-time horse saddles, the sabers and guns. They held meetings, gave lectures at schools and performed re-enactments at Greenfield Village.

But their group had no home. So when the old horse stables became available to them three years ago, along with a lot of office space they didn't need, they put together a historical exhibit dedicated to their heroes and opened it to the public.

The exhibit's displays are small and few so far. A cabinet holds some historical items, such as pictures and documents. An old saddle rests on a stand next to an easel holding a board featuring yellowed news articles. Trophies line a set of shelves, prizes from parades the group marched in over the years.

There are no official tours, other than when Buchanan shows horse riders around.

"People walk inside and look at the showcase and ask, 'What's going on?' and then that gives us the opportunity to talk about it," he says.

The Buffalo Soldiers Calico Troops, as his group calls itself, is down to four members. Death and the economy have taken their toll. They've tried to recruit, but the uniforms are expensive, and in tough times, few people have that kind of money for this kind of hobby. They've resorted to a slightly ghoulish solution and give new members pre-worn costumes. "A lot of the guys who have passed away, we've been using their uniform to patch up," he says.

Those uniforms still grab the attention of the kids they speak to at city schools. Their interest, though, is often for the wrong reasons.

"Of course, the first question they always ask is what kind of gun do you carry," Buchanan says, "and they can almost tell me as much about the weapon I have as I can. And we're speaking of grade school kids."

But when his group goes to a classroom, dressed in the blues and grays of the Buffalo Soldiers, all eyes are on them. And when Buchanan sings the Buffalo Soldiers anthem, his voice the lone sound hanging in the air, the students are fascinated.

"A lot of our young black kids, the only thing they know about our history is that we were slaves," he says. "And it's very demeaning to them. But we like to tell these kids that all black men was not slaves, that there were black cowboys and blacks in Congress in the 1880s, that there were famous young black men during those depressive times. And they did their job very well."

BUCHANAN FELL IN love with horses the first time he saw them on his grandfather's tobacco farm in Tennessee.

"I used to climb a fence, and the horse walked by and I'd grab it by the mane and jump on. That darn horse, it would actually take care of me, because I would start to slide off and it would stop and wait for me to adjust myself and he'd walk again."

He became infatuated. Didn't even have to be a real horse to capture his attention. "Mom used to take me to Kresge's and she made sure she had a couple dimes for that old pony you used to put the coins in," he says, laughing. "I had the horse bug at that point."

Kids from the city, he finds, are just as fascinated by horses today as he was at their age.

Madison Reid, age three, rides a horse inside Detroit's city limits.

"Sometimes they're afraid because they're bigger than they thought, and there's other times they're gung-ho, just jumping up there. But usually the ones that's afraid, once they get up there, we have just as much trouble getting them off." Rides cost four dollars for once around the fence, six dollars to go twice.

"This is the greatest thing ever," says Ranada Reid, thirty-five, as her three-year-old daughter, Madison, rides a horse around the corral, "'cause I wouldn't be able to afford to go get her lessons. She fantasizes about horses. We're in the middle of Detroit, so we don't see horses, but she sees them on TV."

James Mills, seventy, saddles a horse nearby. "They understand what you're thinking," he says about his horse. He loves them as much as Buchanan does. "They trust you as much as you trust them."

Sometimes, as the day ends, when everyone leaves, he and Buchanan will saddle up and ride their horses around the woods and fields, looking much like their icons, who probably never dreamed that, a century later, some strangers would wear their uniforms and tell their story.

"The original soldiers did not get the proper respect that they were supposed to have or should have gotten," Buchanan says. "Better late than never."

Desolation Angel

A Bank-Robbing Preacher Leads a Flock of Addicts and Hookers
Straight Out of Detroit's Gutters

THEY STAGGER IN one by one—each with a story, each with a life of problems.

First comes the prostitute. Then comes a drinker. Every swing of the door brings another desperate person from the street outside.

People with addictions, with diseases, people living on the street. And people who suffer from none of those things but who are just drawn to this strange place.

Some talk to each other; one or two are talking to themselves, or the air, or whatever demons they hear in their heads.

It's Sunday morning. It's time for church.

At Peacemakers International on Chene Street, a little storefront ministry not far south of I-94, the congregation doesn't just help people who are addicts or poor or homeless. Those people are the congregation.

They come here because this place has taken in dozens of people fighting years of addiction, and somehow, they say, it has helped them get off drugs. People like Tony Cusmano, fifty-two, who gradually stole a quarter-million dollars from his family business to feed a cocaine habit before ending up behind bars. Like Shirley Robinson, fifty-three, who gave up a career and a house for a coke habit, which became a crack habit that left her selling herself on this street for a few years. Like Coy Welch, thirty-nine, a longtime drinker who was found living under a bridge a couple months ago and was invited to come here.

And from this ragged crowd, the preacher emerges.

At first it's hard to distinguish him from his flock. Steve Upshur is sixty-two and wears jeans and cowboy boots and a leather Harley jacket. His hair is long. So is his scraggly mustache. He's a biker and looks like a biker.

He used to be an addict, so desperate he once puked up his methadone at a clinic and then got down on the ground to lap up the drug-soaked vomit. He's been a dealer. He's been jailed. He even got caught up in a bank robbery once.

His flock relates to him because he's been where they are, because he's done as much wrong in his life as they have in theirs, but more importantly because he's someone who found a way out of that hell. He's walked the walk. And because of that, he's earned their trust, earned his post as father of the wayward.

"When you get into crack and prostitution, anything goes," Upshur says. "A lot of these people will stuff people in trunks, kill people. I've had people confess murders in here. I've heard it all."

More people arrive. A homeless man. A woman one misstep away from being there. An old lady with a scowling face, muttering to herself.

The services begin right on time. But there's no prayer to start things off. No reading of the Bible. No sermon.

Instead, a high-tempo, old-time gospel song—"I Believe" by John P. Kee—blares from the stereo. And as the beat kicks in, everyone in the pews who had been sitting quietly suddenly gets up and starts clapping along. A few even dance.

Then the pastor says a few short words, but right away another song bursts out of the stereo, and the congregation is behaving like it's some kind of dance party. People who were living on the street or still are, people selling themselves there, people crippled by drug and drinking problems, are all dancing together, looking like they haven't had this kind of fun in years. It's an astonishing sight.

And just when it seems this can't possibly be the actual service, it turns out that this is indeed how it goes at Peacemakers. Down here on Chene, going to Sunday service is almost like going to a party where, for a couple hours, the weight of everyone's troubled pasts falls away.

"It's just upbeat, you know?" Upshur says. "This isn't a dead place where everybody's sitting there. That ain't the way a church is supposed to be."

Pastor Steve Upshur, on his motorcycle, surrounded by members of his flock.

CHENE STREET IS a disaster. The rows of burned-out storefronts between the empty blocks are reminders of how bustling it once was. But after the 1967 riot, after the freeway and an auto plant split the neighborhood in half, after everyone packed up and moved away, almost everything just died off.

Pouring into the void left behind were outcasts and cast-asides—junkies and drunks, hookers and drug dealers, the mentally ill and the physically disabled. Like a few other areas of the city, it became a refuge of the underclass, a home for everyone with nowhere else to go, where they can wander freely without being chased away by store owners or told to move along by the cops.

"It's like the devil's playground," says John Simon, a minister here. "I mean, you got sexual acts in the middle of the day, shooting dope, smoking dope. Everything you can imagine is going on down here."

This is the world in which Peacemakers established itself in 1994. In many ways it's a typical inner-city, grass-roots church. The services are nondenominational and loose. And like any Christian ministry, the place seeks to create believers and followers in Jesus, though they give food and clothing to anyone who comes here, whether they profess a belief in God or not.

But something's happening here that draws the people who work or live on the streets outside. Just about every member swears that sometime after they came here, there was a moment when everything changed for them, when their addictions simply vanished. Whether what took place for them was spiritual or psychological, whether the catalyst was from inside or out, the simple program offered here, they say, helped alter their lives. It's not a twelve-step program, more a strict combination of work, prayer and study that uses religious belief to shield against the temptation for an addict to return to his or her old life.

Maybe Peacemakers gives a template to people who've never had a code of behavior to guide them. Maybe some people just need a strict system of rules to follow. Either way, its members insist that this place works.

A whole system has evolved to support them, a virtual safety net in a neighborhood that never really had one. The church operates halfway houses for ex-cons and ex-prostitutes, sets up gardens for flowers and vegetables and keeps a chicken coop for eggs. It all goes to the neighborhood. And every day, members give out food and clothes.

This place is often the last resort for neighborhood people whose choices or circumstances left them living on the lowest rungs. The program offered here is powerful and appealing because it's so simple.

"The main thing is a sincere desire to find God and get your life together, and a willingness to stick to the rules," says Jeremiah Upshur, the pastor's thirty-two-year-old son.

Those rules require members to be sober, to pray together and to participate in helping the poor by feeding, clothing and working to get them off the streets. But a stated belief in Jesus is not enough to stay here. They have to demonstrate those convictions with the people of Chene Street.

"It's a hard ministry. The hardest thing that I've ever done in my entire life is to be a Christian," Simon says of the work involved. "But it's the most fulfilling."

After Peacemakers opened, the street people out front saw their old friends suddenly sober, talking about this crazy church that's feeding and clothing them and helping them get clean, even if sometimes it doesn't last, and they began showing up out of curiosity. Soon, its reputation took on a life of its own, and strange things started happening.

"We would have fires in this giant fire pit back there, and people would be coming in, throwing their syringes in, throwing their crack pipes in, just giving it all up," Simon says. "It was mind-blowing."

THE PASTOR GOT here the long, hard way. He was a juvenile delinquent who became a teenage heroin addict. Petty crimes grew into bigger ones until he found himself nodding off at the wheel of a bank robbery getaway car one afternoon in the early '70s in Detroit's suburbs, just as the cops swarmed in. He barely escaped lengthy prison time for it.

He fled Detroit but kept his lifestyle. While in an Oklahoma jail in the early '70s for some minor offense, an inmate told him these born-again Christians had a place nearby, and they could be easily suckered into giving you food and shelter. "So I'm thinking, 'Well, go get me a sandwich; I'll go hustle them for a sandwich,'" Upshur says.

But he was drawn in by their approach. "These people are talking to Jesus like he's their buddy, and I grew up you'd have to probably be a priest or a nun to be talking firsthand to the main man," says Upshur, who was raised Catholic. "I'm thinking this is deep. All of a sudden—boom!—this spiritual world opens up. I'm like, 'You gotta be kidding me.'"

He was so inspired, he came back to Detroit at twenty-five years old, determined to stay clean, and started holding informal prayer meetings at a house next to his parents' home to talk about spirituality or God or whatever anyone wanted. At the first gathering, his audience was a bunch of teenagers who came less to hear another born-again and more to see the crazy bank robber. A week later, he had thirty-five kids there. Soon after, adults started showing up too.

The group kept growing and went from a house to an old, unused church in Detroit and eventually to a church in St. Clair Shores with three pastors and a large middle-class congregation. Upshur preached out there for sixteen years.

But he felt the pull of skid row. "That's always where my heart was, 'cause I come out of that," he says. "I grew up in the inner city, I've been homeless many of the years of my life, been in and out of jail all my life, a very rough life. Those were my main people that I grew up with. So when I got, quote, 'saved,' I knew I'd be back working with people that come out of my environment."

A woman in the suburban church offered him a small old building on Chene that she owned, and he began his ministry in one of the city's most miserable, drug-addled neighborhoods. "We take people who everybody else has given up on," Bob Kaczmarek says. He's a board member of the church, sixty-four, a Catholic, a well-dressed attorney. He attends services elsewhere but was so impressed by Peacemakers and its ragged flock he became involved.

"This is it," he says. "For some of the people who are in the in-house programs, this is their last chance. And if they don't make it here, then you find out they're found dead somewhere."

THERE HAVE TO be at least one hundred stuffed animals inside the bedrooms at the Mercy House.

Several women stay here right now, at the Peacemakers' halfway house for those trying to escape a life of prostitution and drugs or battered women trying to escape violent men. Blocks away, there's a halfway house for men out of prison, off the streets, just off drugs.

What's striking about the women's house are the delicate, feminine, almost child-like touches. Though the women here have led hard lives, there's pink and softness everywhere—on the stuffed animals, in the decorations on the walls, on the clothes inside the closets. It's as if the women here are trying to reclaim an innocence they lost years ago. Denise Benn walks into her bedroom, bounces onto her bed and grabs a blue stuffed dog. "I got this puppy I took care of right before I came in here, and it made me feel young again, 'cause I could take care of something," the forty-three-year-old says, hugging it.

Benn's history is written on her face. Her story is like one many of the women here tell. Her life collapsed at twelve, she says, when she was gang raped by six men on the way to school. Soon after, she started doing drugs to bury the trauma, hanging out with the dropouts and the druggies because they were nicer to her than anyone else.

"I liked getting high," she says. "People accepted me. I wasn't part of my family because I didn't get along with my family. But now I was part of something."

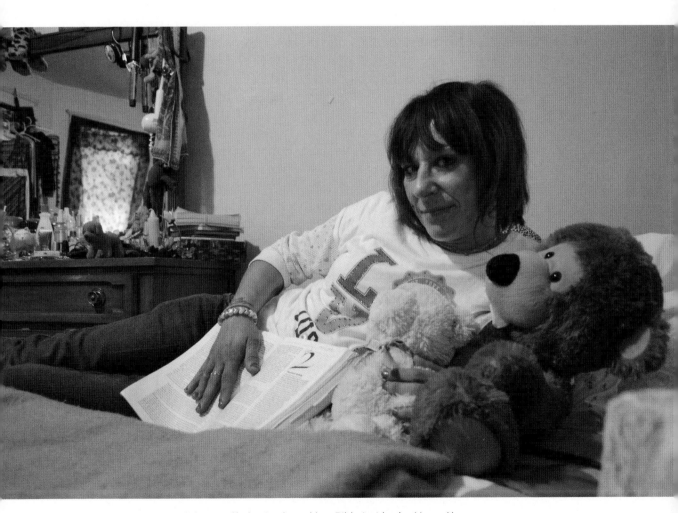

Denise Benn with her stuffed animals and her Bible inside the Mercy House.

By sixteen, she was pole dancing in Detroit strip clubs, strung out on heroin, and within a couple years she went from turning tricks in VIP rooms to doing so in cars.

Her life as a street prostitute was one harrowing night after another.

"Every day something horrific was happening to me," she says. "I was either getting thrown out of moving cars or waking up with people's hands on my throat, and I had a heroin addiction and I couldn't stop. I mean, you should see the scars on my body. I'm not lying to you. I've had some horrific stuff happen to me."

The women here—five right now—watch out for each other, keep each other's spirits up when things look bleak and the street outside begins appearing appealing again. They travel in twos when they walk the neighborhood, and eat group dinners, and help out at the church together.

"I got a new way of life," Benn says. "I'm productive here and I'm of use here. I've got a place here."

But there are relapses here too.

Last spring she violated the rules against dating someone at a nearby halfway house for men and, forced to leave, wound up back on the streets, living in an abandoned building.

"The first night I went there, I just cried, because I knew what was going to happen," Benn says. She fell right back into drugs and prostitution. "I didn't have nowhere to go. I didn't have no resources. I didn't have a dime in my pocket."

Jeremiah Upshur, the pastor's son, came looking for her and asked her to come back. Now she works for the church and tries to figure out how to build a new life. She has no money, can't even get past a minimum-wage job interview because of the long gap in her work history and has few skills other than the ones she picked up on the streets. It makes it tough to stay hopeful, challenging to remain on the path she's trying to follow.

"It's hard," Benn says, dragging on a cigarette. "It's really hard."

IT ALL COMES down to a single moment, they say. A line between their old lives and their new one. And they all say it like they still half can't believe it actually happened.

Two congregants from the streets outside listen to the preacher.

It happened to Simon too. He tells his story as he wanders the aisles at Joseph's Storehouse, the church's resale shop in Warren that he runs. This is where the church gets what little money it has—selling cheap things one or two at a time.

Simon's one of Peacemakers' biggest proponents because he's one of its biggest successes.

He'd already spent half a life on heroin, a habit he began at fifteen, when he first came here.

"I must've did $400, $500 worth of heroin every day, 'cause that was my daily do," he says. "My lottery habit was a hundred and something a day, the cocaine I used to give out for free was hundreds a day. I literally had tons of weed. I was hooked up with these Cubans and Colombians in Florida. And I was the dope man, so I had some of the finest women God put breath in. I was out of my mind. It was just a big party continuously."

He got conned into coming to Peacemakers by a concerned sister who'd heard this place seems to work when everything else fails.

Simon walked in, thinking he'd bail after a minute, but he found a remarkable scene that had him transfixed.

"First time I went down there, I just felt something," he says. "Jeremiah, the pastor's son, was standing in the middle of the kitchen with all these dope fiends and prostitutes just standing in a circle around him. And I knew these people 'cause I used to be down on Chene."

Simon started attending services but kept showing up wasted. He had to take $100 worth of heroin just to get into

Anthony Mitchell inside the Jesus House, the church's halfway house for men.

the door without being sick. He was listening to the spiritual messages but not the sobriety ones.

"I always heard you get saved and the ground's gonna shake and lightning bolts, and I didn't feel nothing. I shook his hand, went out in the car and got high," he says, laughing.

One day, much to Simon's discomfort, Upshur called him to the floor in the middle of the service. Simon had three bottles of methadone in his pocket. He was able to get them even while he was on heroin because the lady who ran the clinic would, for five dollars, give addicts a cup of her teenage daughter's urine so they could pass the drug test and get their fix. That was her hustle on the side. She kept them addicted for five dollars here and there.

The pastor asked Simon if he wanted to finally be free of drugs. Simon nervously said yes, pulled out the bottles and set them on the pulpit in an act of renouncement. The addicts in the audience started drooling over them.

"You know the crowd on Chene," he says. "I heard, 'Don't do it, John! I'll buy it!' People were serious. These are drug addicts in the crowd. Each bottle could be fifty dollars or more on the street. There's people literally hollering like it's an auction. They want my drugs."

Like so many others here, from the pastor on down, he insists the spirit entered into him that day and his addiction vanished right then and there. No withdrawals, no cravings. That was twelve years ago.

"I went to meetings, NA, AA, methadone clinics, whatever they have. Nothing worked for me," he says. Now he's a minister here trying to do the same for others who come in. "God set me free that day. Everything stopped that day."

JADA FIELDS SITS alone in a pew on a Sunday morning, staring forward without an expression. And tears are streaming down her face.

She was a crack-smoking prostitute working Chene down the street from the church, waiting for johns to pick her up one day, and Upshur called her over. She told him flat-out what she was doing. He offered her money to instead come inside. "I've been here ever since," Fields says. She has nine children, seven grandchildren. She's thirty-nine.

That was eight years ago, eight years of relapses, of going back to the streets and then being welcomed back to Peacemakers. This time she's lasted a year here.

Behind her, a man stands there alone, and he too is crying to himself. Across the room, moments later, a man has his face buried in his hands, in tears or in shame.

This happens early in their newfound sobriety, some here will say, when the remorse of a wasted life sinks in. There's joy in starting over, but there's deep sadness too over all the time that's been lost forever. Sometimes the realization is overwhelming.

But now a song interrupts their sorrow as the service begins. Once again the song is gospel, so raw it has no music backing it at all, only a quick beat driven by foot stomps and a tambourine and carried by the raspy voice of its impassioned singer.

Everyone rises and starts clapping along. Some dance or jump up and down in place. An elderly man shadowboxes the air for lack of another way to express his emotions. A few people come to the front and start dancing in tandem, like they're doing the Hustle. The party's on.

As each song fades away, Upshur says a few things into a microphone. They're not so much religious exhortations, more like a pep talk. "Now we know we all come out of different backgrounds, all kinds of craziness, we all got a story to tell," he tells them. They shout in agreement. His manner is gentle, his tone is soothing. No yelling, no fiery eyes. "But we're gonna help one another cross that finish line, whatever it takes. We're draggin' one another through them pearly gates!"

Though the Gospels will be read aloud toward the end, though there's no doubt this is a religious gathering, the services here are more like a celebration of everyone's escape from their own hell, whether they've done it yet or are still trying. It's a sing- and dance-along that, more than anything, is meant to cheer up people who've had little to smile about.

John Simon inside Joseph's Storehouse, the church's resale shop.

Opposite: The pastor preaches to a raucous full house.

The women of the Mercy House. At left is the pastor's daughter.

"Let's have a knock-down, drag-out for Jesus!" Upshur shouts excitedly as everyone starts dancing to another song. "Let it all hang out!"

Every week, the service stops midway through for a hug break, of all things. But it's actually more striking than corny. Few who come here have families, most have few real friends. So prostitutes turn to hug alcoholics with tremors, and the mentally ill embrace the homeless. Five minutes of everyone melting into one another's arms.

Kaczmarek thinks back to something he saw recently at one of the services. "One fellow got up and said he was thankful because, for the first time in his memory, he feels that he has a family, that he is loved, that he is able to love others who will receive it. From my perspective, that was the best moment of the evening to hear something like that."

These troubled people, holding onto one another in this little room in the ghetto, have created their own safe, protected world here, where they can have friends who won't pull drugs out of their pocket or have liquor on their breath. They're convinced something miraculous can happen to them here, even if it takes a bank-robbing preacher and a flock of addicts and hookers to help them do it.

"It all works somehow," Kaczmarek says, smiling. "Isn't that amazing?"

About the Author

A NATIVE OF Detroit, John Carlisle has written about and photographed the city for the *Metro Times* for four years under the name Detroitblogger John, a pen name based on his long-standing web project, detroitblog. He has also been a contributor to *Hour Detroit* magazine and an editor at the C&G Newspapers chain. A graduate of Wayne State University's journalism program, Carlisle has won numerous awards over the years for his writing and photography and was named Journalist of the Year in 2011 by the Detroit chapter of the Society of Professional Journalists.

Author photograph by Cybelle Codish.

Visit us at
www.historypress.net

———

www.detroitblog.org